MEMOIRS OF A RUM-RUNNER

&

The Life of Clemente de la Cuadra

Memoirs of a Rum-Runner

Based on a true story

Don Clemente de la Cuadra y Gibaja

Translated from the Spanish with additions by
Steven Nelson

Pathways Publishing Ltd

ISBN 978-0-9912538-0-7

For the next generations

He had a strong build, neither tall nor short; upright, majestic, with somewhat of a gut and a head on his shoulders. This is how Don Clemente looks in the middle of the plaza, one foot forward, one hand in his pocket, guarding Utrera. His body made of bronze and rusted over, with a green film over the metal which only time can impart, he stands out and can be seen from anywhere in town.

If we look at him from in front, the way you always have to look at people, we'll meet the entrepreneurial Don Clemente, who never gave up a fight, always looking for greater challenges, a leader of men. If we look at him from behind, the way so many insist on looking at him, maybe we'll see the mafioso, the smuggler, the greedy man...it's the price you have to pay in this world if you were a great person, the heads and tails of the same coin, mirroring and forever following those whose names live beyond death.

From in front we'll look at him!

Don Clemente was born the 23rd of November, 1803 in the Rasines province of Santander, Spain. One among eleven children, the commotion must have obviously influenced the course of his destiny. Of all the siblings, we only know about Francisco Javier, Saturnina, Feliciana, Clemente (of whom we're speaking about) and the younger Jose.

The Cuadra family had always lived in Ampuero, small town close to Rasines, likewise important for being the village where the Gibajas sprang from. The families would ally with the marriage of Doña Manuela Gibaja to Don Juan de la Cuadra, father of Don Clemente. The close proximity must've made it simple enough for our ancestors to meet one another, and this would be the first time that both surnames would be found together at the same time, and the first time that a Cuadra went to live outside of Ampuero, to that village of Rasines.

Two days after his birth, on the 25th of November, Don Clemente was baptized in the missionary church of Saint Andres. The sacrament was conferred by a brother of his mother, Don Tomas, who at the time was partially supported by that same church. There's a curious note surrounding his godparents, his sister Saturnina and Don Rodrigo Crespo, having had to take the place of the intended godparents, his maternal aunt and uncle. She found herself in Utrera and he in Mexico. It was precisely these two points around which Don Clemente would focus his life. It's as if fate had already chosen then and a mysterious hand had written these two places in the baby's soul.

Around that time there was an infectious desire to go to the New World. Some strange mix of ambition, ingenuity and foolhardiness. It was a desire hard to shake off because it appealed to the deep idealism of man, the almost boyish conviction that they had been born to triumph over the world. America was a great land to follow your dreams, as happens with everything that is seen from afar. Thus it shouldn't seem strange that any father with the slightest connection to America would send his sons there. Practically every son born after the firstborn in Ampuero or Rasines or anywhere nearby was born with his suitcase packed up and a passage in his hand. Seeing as how several of his relatives had already followed this path, Don Francisco, Don Agustin, and Don Manuel; brothers of his maternal grandmother, and Don Manuel Viya de Gibaja and Don Francisco de Gibaja had all planted the seeds of adventure for the next generation once they returned rich. This only confirmed the belief that sons were to make their way in the New World, which meant the unappreciated and risky job of being an immigrant.

But Don Clemente carried in his blood the audacity and courage of heroes; men who could not be daunted or dismayed. Men like him could never be placated by the small patch of farm land that his parents owned in the Santander mountains. Small pasture land for livestock like the rest of the folk around Rasines. The longing to be more had probably grown and matured deep in his heart as a reflection of the countless dreams and desires of his ancestors flowing into him. Thus, barely having turned thirteen years old, Don Juan, his father, decided it was time to send him to America. Many years later Don Clemente would give us his tale; we don't know if someone asked him about it in order to go back in time to relive their own youths, or to fill an insatiable hunger to hear a story like his.

"Among all my siblings," says Don Clemente "by the good grace of divine providence, I have ended up being luckiest among those who have made it to old age; Saturnina, who married Don Damaso Vega, passed away, already having been a widow after a long and painful sickness, leaving five children orphaned and under my protection. Jose, my younger brother, died when he was thirty years old just when life was starting to become favorable, and Feliciana who lives near me with her rather large family, never lacked toil and trouble, until I believe, she could rest assured that she could live the last third of her life in rest and tranquility, and reap the fruits knowing she had found favorable positions and spouses for most of her children.

Since I was little my parents sent me to grammar school, supported by the nobles Don Andres Gil de la Torre y Don Francisco de Gibaja, uncles of mine, and the second one brought to the school Don Manuel Bustillos, elementary school teacher of a lot of fame, seeing as how he had taught the grand majority of students from Gibaja, Ampuero, Limpias, Velalla, and Ojebar. He also taught Santiago and Simon, sons of Don Francisco, my uncle.

During the first classes, I went out of my way to show insubordination and be mischievous; and without the healthy force with which I was always corrected, I would have turned out disastrous. However, several episodes which even to this day some neighbors still refer to, and even I remember, show some wit and ingeniousness and that I wasn't without courage and confidence. To illustrate this point I shall give two examples.

In front of our house lived a widowed lady, and in her living room with her children I found myself playing one Sunday while my family had gone to Mass. One of the boys who was with me yelled from the balcony 'Here comes Father Peace!' who was a layman, an almoner from San Francisco de Laredo, and people said of him that he would steal away children whose hands were dirty. Since I happened to be suffering from this defect at the time, and the monk surprised us showing up suddenly, I grabbed the shotgun that was sitting in one of the corners of the living room, and shot at him point-blank. Divine providence saved him, because the gun was heavy and I wasn't strong enough to aim right. The monk escaped taking off running with his robes pulled up, screaming all kinds of obscenities, causing a scandal in town, of which I should have regretted.

Another time, looking for animal nests, I found a rifle that my father had hidden in the hollow of an old chestnut tree, and with it I setup on top of a mound of dirt behind our house. At that time, three or four mule-men strolled by with their droves and carts, and having said to them in a loud voice 'has the mule given birth?', which back then as today is a grave insult to mule-men, who turned and came at me in a rage, while I, without hesitation, lifted the deadly instrument towards them, pointing the barrel at them, and screamed at them with a firm voice 'if you come one step closer I'll kill you!' At that moment my father showed up and what happened afterwards anyone can figure out.

However it happened, by force or on my own, by the time I was eleven I could read, write and count well enough, which was just about all you would learn in school back then. My honorable father then moved me to the house of an established businessman in Laredo, who occupied me either as a secretary or with household chores, often making me suffer for one reason or another, his violent and impetuous personality. My new boss, however, showed me many times affection with lots of challenges. First he made me study grammar with him, and later on navigation, until around the end of 1816 my esteemed father arranged to send me to New Spain.

The voyage was in and of itself a dangerous proposition. Frequent attacks by land-based pirates endangered even the best defended expeditions. Since I'd embarked on a sixty ton vessel, we passed unnoticed to those prying eyes who must've thought we were a coal-ship from among the islands, and we arrived well. After sixty-some days of sailing, having suffered strong winds and storms, including a north wind that they call 'the Bad Cheese', we made it to the Mexican coastline.

Upon my arrival in Veracruz, I was met by my honorable uncle Don Manuel and his family, who showered me with unending attention during the month that I stayed in their home. Afterwards I was on my way to the capital in an armed convoy, as the whole countryside was in revolt, despite the extraordinary measures adopted by Viceroy Don Juan Ruiz de Apodaca, who couldn't quite suppress it.

I spent two years in Mexico (1817-1818). The first was in the famous clothing shop run by Don Francisco de Herreras, hailing from Santander. The second one, at the desk of Don Barenque, from Rasines, from the Lambera neighborhood, who inaugurated my fortune by blessing me with a salary of one hundred silver nickels a year.

Señor Barenque was a successful gentleman whose fatherly attention, both his advice and reprimands, made me forget the inconsiderate treatment I went through in the house of Señor Herreras by the other employees there. Ten years later I would have the pleasure of bailing out some of the more arrogant workers and Herreras himself, after being deported from the Republic of the United States for their multitude of blunders.

Unfortunately the house of Señor Barenque underwent hard times that made him lose clout in the world of business. At the same time, he sent me to the Valley of San Francisco, twelve miles from San Luis Potosi, even though it pained me greatly to leave what I considered my home. Who would've known that years later I would find his only daughter in Cadiz, a beautiful girl, educated in all the subjects, turn up at my doorstep for relief from her poverty.

I spent the whole year of 1820 in the Valley of San Francisco, working in a type of store called a mestiza, where they sell clothes, and serve drinks and meals. But since nothing there offered me what I knew was my destiny, neither the lack of commerce, nor did anyone renowned live there, I was easily swayed by the promises of glory by a native of the land, who resided high in the mountains in Real de Catorce, who brought me there with his group.

Around this time, Odonoju and several other Spanish generals betrayed their father land and helped Iturbide in his insurrection and the consummation of Mexican independence. The damage to my fatherland happened right away but the aforementioned generals had their fate decided another day. God would surely want their repugnant ingratitude to suffer later by another repugnant betrayal.

Arriving at Real de Catorce, it didn't take me long to see that my boss had his head wound up in all kinds of illusions with little grasp of reality. His business revolved around selling clothing to the beneficiaries of the local silver mines. There was a limit to what his skills could do, and my boss had fallen to that fever that takes over all men who become obsessed with silver mines, strangling him with false hopes and backstabbing.

It's not hard to understand that being around this type of sick individual would bring about its share of trouble. Surely if you had lived in that kind of a town you would understand, even one in Spain, that being a miner and a visionary were one in the same. I fell prey to the dreams of those more passionate about this than me, and I spent the majority of the year 1821 between 700 and 800 yards underground; exploring and testing, and acting rather imprudently which quite frequently compromised my existence. The only reward that came out of all this was that I had wasted a lot of time and money.

This failure coincided with the death of the wife of my boss, who was a friendly and good woman, and also the future heiress of some great fortune. Seeing my boss plan out his financial future, because his father-in-law still lived and they had no other heirs, he decided that we should head off to Mazapil, trying to get away from the strict rules of the political class to which he would have to be obedient. Once we'd arrived there, we happened to cross paths with another joker, who managed to bring about once again our excitement for mining, who finally convinced me to stay at the Hacienda de Cedros and dedicate myself to working in one particular mine we called 'the Cave'. But once my boss came back from Parras, where he had gone to rent some equipment, we looked at our ledger and turned out that instead of profits we had losses. And since it turned out that I was a business partner of his, I ended up being in debt for some amount that I'd never even spent. Thus ended our relationship in which I would have never involved myself with if they hadn't tricked me and made me believe that I was going to be owner of villas and castles and the owner of a solvent business that never existed.

In the mine 'the Cave' I buried my last hopes. And after my business partner disappeared for ever, like magic, I had no other choice but to return to the Valle de Matehuala, where I stayed with his father-in-law, Don Marcos de la Puente, originally from Ruesga.

Having worked as an assistant in the store of the honorable Don Marcos, an incident occurred that I'll tell you of now, if for no other reason than to record the hard lesson learned from what appeared to be an innocent indiscretion: an old Spaniard named Cosgaya used to come every day to the store who had the habit of asking us for a drink, of course always with the permission of Señor Don Marcos, who liked him a lot. Well, one day we had the bad luck of sprinkling in some wood dust, which is a very powerful laxative that the indigenous people here make. The recipient drank the wine without noticing anything, leaving a while later good and healthy like always. But at three in the afternoon, more or less, a doctor ran by us saying that they'd urgently called him from his home. The man had found himself attacked by an extraordinary diarrhea.

Naturally we understood right away the gravity of our actions, after all. We were thinking how we would evade the inevitable consequences to ourselves, when all of a sudden the church bells tolled. At that point there was no choice but to go as fast as possible to the sick man's house, come out and confess what we did and supply the man with the cold *Atole*, the known antidote for that kind of venom. I had made myself in charge of recounting our horrid deed, and I learned with glee and surprise, upon arriving at the man's dwelling, the man we'd thought dead, that the church bells did not signal his death but rather that of an even greater afflicted man, and I suffered the abuses and reproach of the family upon making my declarations. The worst part was that the whole episode became common knowledge and the talk of the town and we were the targets of a lot of sarcasm for quite a few days. Amen that my patron dished out the deserved punishment, not withstanding that the old man later fully recovered.

The respectable Señor Gomez de la Puente thought so highly of me after not having been at his service for long, so much that he made me the administrator in charge of his estate at Pastoriza. I was barely even eighteen years old and I ventured without the knowledge and prudence that comes with experience. He made sure I omitted nothing; to make sure my work was reliable while I managed his interests during those two years. And apart from a few small improprieties, he had no reason to regret it. But his wife, proud and foolish, who also dominated him, used to like start rumors and always felt it necessary to harass the workers. Seeing as how it wasn't in my character to put up with such vilification I felt the need to leave the position to my assistant who had already found himself tied up in the aforementioned drama as well as for other, more indignant, reasons.

From Matehuala, I left for Tampico de Tamaulipas, that was being built around that time (1823), and I owed no small amount of gratitude to Don Jose and Don Fermin de la Lastra who lived in Altamira and Pueblo Viejo, located near each other.

In Tampico I stayed long enough to convince myself that there was no position there that I wanted, and I left for Tuspam, that same year 1823, looking for the protection of Don Juan del Juncal, who occupied an advantageous position there. And sure enough, he received me in his house with the same affection he would show to someone just born.

Almost immediately Juncal sent me to Veracruz as shipmate of one of his cargo vessels (the *San Cayetano*), in order to receive a shipment, in said place, of fruit that it carried and to return afterwards with the goods having been converted into money. The mission accomplished, I returned to everyone's satisfaction, but bad fortune wished upon me that during the business exchange in the narrow sea inlet of Tuspam, they hurled a bale of goods from the gunwale when they were loading, and it flipped over the canoe that I was in and I fell into the cold water. Afterwards I caught a fever that lasted until the end of 1824.

During this unfortunate time period, the most pathetic of my life, the suffering and privations reached the extreme. It's true that Señor Juncal never failed to give me the deserved care; whenever I felt able I would make myself useful by managing the ledgers of his business, and later when there was a new store opening, he sent me to manage it and I carried out the task flawlessly. But one day, feeling desperate about my health, I took off to Campeche to look for relief by changing the temperature around me, and not only did he not compensate me for my management of his store, but he also charged me for the costs incurred while I was sick and even the little that I had borrowed to make the trip.

Once again I embarked anew, and the ordeal was so difficult that more than once the results brought me to the gates of death and the merchant thought it prudent to drop me off upon arrival in Campeche and intern me in the hospital of San Juan de Dios to spend there the last remaining hours of my existence.

Upon my internment at that establishment, instantly Don Pedro Manuel Rodriguez came to visit me, originally from a town called Arnuero, of whom he was the merchant who did business there. Since he was an honorable man and a generous man, and my youth and visage enchanted him, he made the top doctor himself come take care of me, who was called Gallegos, who confirmed that my diagnosis was fatal and that any medical care would be useless.

This not withstanding, he administered to me some spiritive drink that revived my senses, and with them the faculty to explain the causes of my ailment, which were not the ones that they had presumed, and instead were ones that had commenced with intermittent fever and continued to reoccur tenaciously over the months, had taken away my appetite and created an invincible repugnance to any and all foods, of any kind. From there my weakness drove me to the deplorable situation in which I found myself.

A black slave took charge of rehabilitating my completely extinguished strength with a soup especially prepared by the doctor. The african discharged his mission fantastically and continually offered me the prodigious sustenance that I got out of religious faith, as apparently during my trance I never lost hope. After twenty four hours I was already another man.

At that time Señor Rodriguez transferred me to the house of some ladies who took charge of taking care of me. They did it very effectively and my convalescence was visible to the naked eye. But bad luck at the time, as during those days the Yucatans, who were at war with the Campechanos, came close to our city and bombed it incessantly. Divine providence at that time exposed me to a new and clear danger.

After the campaign ended, I found myself much more fit and with a pair of crutches I was skipping around the grounds. And before two months passed I decided to return straight to Tuspan.

I attributed my ungodly recovery to a frightful resolution I had taken. During the depression I felt myself in as a consequence of the intensity and obstinacy of the suffering, my arms and legs became crippled. To the point that I'd had to be fed by a stranger's hand. In this lamentable state, the head doctor paid me a normal visit, and after the questions about my strength and having spent some time with me, he went right away to the next room over, where the nurses were, they interrogated him over my health, wishing to know whether they could maintain hope of my recovery, and he simply said: 'For God, nothing is impossible.'

I heard this mistake, and I called for him. When he was before me again I told him: 'To get healthy, if God wishes, I don't need you. I hope that you won't visit me anymore. I want you to know that I won't take anything that you prescribe me because I'm convinced that you know nothing of what ails me, and before continuing to suffer by trusting in your ignorance, I'd rather trust in Divine Providence even if I succumb to this illness.'

Then, the man muttered something, and responded to my harsh words by taking off, irritated like a madman. I kept on by refusing the concoctions that the doctor had tried to heal me with, all for naught. Neither the pleadings of the owners, nor the advice and reprimands of the concocter, nor the prudent observations of other people, were enough to make me give up my resolve. From that moment on, renouncing every medicine, I did nothing more than sustain myself with whatever foods appealed to me the most. Then, I started exercising and training as soon as I felt better, making fun of the false prophets, determined to start my journey to the continent.

Determined, I tell you, I loaded my baggage in the schooner *San Cayetano* belonging to Juncal. But, a couple hours before we set off, the same Captain that had taken me to Campeche showed up. And delighted to find me alive, he insisted unconditionally that I make the trip on his ship instead. I resisted as much as I could since I had everything already on board, but, without asking permission, he had his servant pick up my bags and he insisted so strongly that I had no choice but to accept. I thus freed myself from a certain death. Without knowing, I had abandoned a ship whose destiny was to wreck during this trip.

In Tuspam, it didn't take me long to recuperate fully, and neither did it take me long to figure out that nothing or next to nothing could prosper in the house of Señor Juncal, as he made sure to monopolize any and all business. I decided then to take a position that a merchant from Pueblo Viejo offered me, and even though the business was quite pitiful, surely due to the unique personality of my new boss, in turn it brought me a decent income that let me save a little. And when I had a thousand nickels, I opted for independence.

With absolute ownership of myself, my first task was, naturally, to choose the means to make myself rich quick. And since the occasion happened to come by me at that moment in Tampico, to buy red wine, that in San Luis de Potosi had an exorbitant price, I decided to purchase fifty barrels, which cost me the previously mentioned sum of money, more or less. And I dispatched them to Don Juan Zabalardo, who was one of the richest dealers at that time with a great network, along with some competent people.

Even though the wine arrived at its destination late and thus deteriorated, I was told that they had sold seven barrels for forty four nickels, which paid for the shipment, the wages and other expenses, and that forty three other barrels waited in storage for another bidder.

Meanwhile, as I awaited the results, giving repeated orders to sell the inventory which were not heeded, when I started to become impatient for want of something to do, at the beginning of 1825, a proposition from Señor Juncal came to distract me. He wanted me to take charge of a shipment of pepper and sarsaparilla that he wanted to ship abroad. As soon as I heard, I took off to Tuspam, I worked day and night to gather the cargo that was valued at over twelve thousand silver nickels, and I followed the orders of Don Jose de Lastra who had legal power from Juncal to act as he saw fit with it. My effort would be compensated with three thousand nickels upon our return. That's to say, with one fourth of the profit that this investment produced. A paltry sum with which my friend thought he was justly compensating me, and which in another situation I would have refused indignantly.

Arriving in New York without incident on the ship *Altamaria* after having spent the March equinox in the ocean, an omen which portented various failings, I sold the cargo at a profit and purchased from the markets there those products I figured to be the most advantageous, I returned with the same merchant ship to Tampico. Furthermore, completely separate from the merchant cargo I had ordered, I carried 2,822 pesos that a merchant had lent me on credit and which Don Francisco de la Maza had guaranteed, that old and good friend.

The expedition had been a total success. Upon our arrival we found the plaza deserted and we were able to conduct our business without problems of any sort. Consequently, the profits were quite handsome, and to my benefit almost three thousand nickels corresponded to me. However, since during my absence Don Juan Zabalardo had embarked to Europe and his brother-in-law whom he had left in charge of his business was just a figurehead who never attended to the assets nor the liabilities, finally it went bankrupt and all the creditors stood mocked and left with nothing, myself among them. And thus I saw disappear, all at once, the bruised dreams of a poor man, the first and most difficult twenty thousand *reales* of my fortune.

This last expedition being complete, Mr. Juncal sent word for me to join him in a new venture that he intended to make to France. Later on, after finding out all I could about fruits, which was the commodity we were dealing with, I did not wish to join this endeavor. He only wished to split one third of the profits with me, and seeing as how it required me to put up all of my money, I would be working for free, more or less. Nevertheless, I continued to work in his home and acted as his representative in his absence.

Meanwhile, some friends of mine organized an expedition from Tuspan, with the pretense of going to the ports of North America, which originally had been headed to Havana, which the (Mexican) Republic was at war with. The job was very risky, but offered some advantages in turn. Since Spanish products were prohibited in Mexican territory and likewise being infinitely desired by the locals, they traded for fabulous prices when one managed to introduce them disguised as foreign products.

These speculators thought of me to be their front man. And notwithstanding the wise observations of those who understood the dangers I exposed myself to, including Mr. Juncal who gave me numerous and strong reasons to dissuade me, including invoking my dreams with the hope that he would make me his business partner one day, I ventured forward without any hesitation, dragged by some secret force that has always led me towards difficult fights.

I gained a favorable salary, and after requesting a loan in order to augment my cargo, I had a salary of 3,200 that was coming to me for completing just one job.

Under these wonderful conditions I marched my way to the island of Cuba on the brigantinee *Hero*. And although I intended to trade separately, I pooled my capital with that of Perez and the others because that way we all benefited more from our purchases; this in spite of the shenanigans they pulled on me at the last minute – it was miserable. But my desire to work and prove myself was enormous.

In Havana, Perez' lack of experience and general idiocy put me in the position of having to do all the trading myself. But it let me select one of the most exquisite cargos for the Mexican markets, and, in the same ship, we headed to customs to present our false papers and present ourselves as Americans. Without the help of one of the Americans on board, Mr. Jones, the entire effort would have been futile.

But in order to do this it was necessary to unload the ship and pay the tariff. At that point we realized that the floor of the ship was completely rotten making it impossible to continue the voyage. But one of the shipbuilders was with me, Galician by birth, called Pepon Perez, who even though he couldn't read was a clever man and very street smart. He told me that with a few repairs we could continue. And to persuade me that we would go on safely, he signed a contract guaranteeing any damages that might happen to the goods on the way back to Mexico. My innocence reigned supreme; it did not let me realize how little we would've cared of such guarantees if we ended up capsizing.

At that moment and from the same port, a schooner called *Antoinette de Pereira* took off destined for Tampico, and I made sure that our papers had the same destination because there was a Colombian Corsair anchored next to us who observed our movements with poorly disguised intentions. Later on I'll explain why.

The *Antoinette* and the *Hero* made off to sea together. The Corsair remained in stream, we followed the schooner and made it to Tuspam even though we had no sea-men except for the Captain who was a total drunk since the pilot had gotten off right before takeoff.

Anchored in port, and it being impossible to leave due to the tide, let's remember that the Captain and Pepon had disembarked in order to fill out some superfluous paperwork for Juncal, which Pepon had hidden in his shoes. I stayed on board in order to direct the unloading on the condition that they verify the paperwork at once and that they send me some fresh food which we lacked since the Galician preferred penny pinching.

Eight days passed without hearing anything from land, and anyone who knows how easy it was to ruin somebody back then for the sole crime of being born a Spaniard; if you had heard of the repugnant activities of the so-called Jauregui, who at the time was a military commander of that district; you would easily understand my anxious situation which foreboded my absolute destruction.

On daybreak of the ninth day, they augmented my fright by several cannon shots coming from the ocean, landing just a short distance from where we floated. Not long after we saw the schooner come closer that had just shouted at us. It was the warship *Papaloapam*, fleeing from Tampico to Veracruz carrying one hundred gunners and twenty six women, and having lost their rudder, they found themselves forced to call for help.

They threw out the anchor and the commander came to speak with me so that we would pick up the passengers. But I managed to only allow the women to board us, as I protested that the soldiers might commit some transgressions on my ship, and seeing as how we were in such proximity to them, it would be easy to come to their aid, if need be. Agreeing to this, and while the females were being transported over, with their luggage, dogs, cats, parrots and all the belongings that accompany Mexican soldiers, on this small boat going back and forth to the *Papaloapam*, while they discussed how to bring the schooner in port to repair it. And in the last trip, at dusk, a man named Roque Garcia, a Mallorcan, came to speak with me. Even though he was half inebriated, he told me frankly, passing by me, that Juncal had sent him to warn me that all was lost and that I should do whatever I wanted.

Surprised by his demeanor and by the way this news arrived to me, I tried to make him explain things to me, but I couldn't get anything out of him other than ,there's no hope at all; the Captain and Pepon are locked in a cell, and if they catch you they will shoot you for sure.'

This news confirmed my fears, and it was now inevitable that my suspicions would come true, I found myself in the desperate situation of a man in a chapel having just been condemned to death. Because, escape was impossible - the villain on land who wanted my demise would surely order the commander of the warship *Papaloapam* to fire on me, even if there were women on board. It didn't even appear rational. And expecting justice or mercy from he who wanted to take my cargo so bad that he would murder me in order to satisfy his disgusting vices, vices which dominated him, would have been crazy. God, who sometimes allows bad people to get away with things to test the faith and resolve of the good, did not intend for the criminal intentions of Jauregui to be realized.

The insomnia caused by my situation gave me such fatigue that I spent the entire night delirious until dawn, spilling her light over the horizon, came to change the scene. The pilot came and told us that the *Papaloapam* had to hold anchor until the tides calmed before entering port. They took the women on shore, relieving me of the greatest burden I had ever felt in my life, and as soon as I began to breathe in a semblance of relief, when the glimmer of a new day's brilliant light began to illuminate my lost cause once again, the naval commander came on board and informed me that they wanted to arrest me on land, and being an employee of that nation, he was in charge of arresting me and placing me before the courts.

By chance, having foreseen such a situation, I received the news with indifference, outwardly at least. Despite the fact that they were going to lock me up, take away my liberty and my greatest dreams, probably forever. I concentrated my faculties and making a supreme effort, guided by necessity, I managed to convince him that he had no need to worry, because I fully intended to present myself to the local authorities the following day. In order to avoid any doubts and to exaggerate the needless efforts he would have to go through, since I found myself under a foreign flag, I managed to dissuade him to wait until tomorrow.

At that moment, hesitating would not suffice. The situation was quite tenuous, and I either had to surrender myself or play this cat and mouse game to perfection. At twenty three years of age and feeling very passionate, the choice that I would take was long ago decided. But without the ship's crew, all would be lost. And since they were all Americans, and the only one I understood was the cook, the black African who spoke English and Spanish, through his intermediation the crew understood that the Captain and the Galician had been imprisoned, and the same fate awaited us all if they caught us. And having painted for them an accurate depiction of the anguish of captivity, I proposed to them that we head off to Tampico to save ourselves, something which they, of course, accepted.

Under these circumstances, when the time came for morning prayer, I invited the commander and all of the naval officers of the *Papaloapam* to tea on our ship. I offered them the best that I had and on top of that there were games and gin, to which they were greatly inclined. My shipmate Mr. Jones assisted in the task. He barely spoke Castilian but was inventing stories on the spot and entertaining the other crew. Assisted by Virgo and Bacchus, I managed to get them all back to their boat, mostly drunk, and I along with them, not before having taken a few bottles with me to finish the job. We drank the most boiling liquor, flushed with hurrahs, and sang the most belligerent patriotic songs, as one after the other began losing consciousness.

Around midnight more or less, I returned to our ship, after first having made sure that all the guards on the *Papaloapam* were sound asleep, taking advantage of the unconsciousness of their bosses. And without wasting a minute, we put the whole crew to work on the task. In silence, we lifted anchor, passed by the warship, covered in fog, we avoided wrecking ourselves on the jagged rocks, they had never looked so big. After two days we had made it to the port of Tampico in record time.

Determined to avoid being boarded, we hoisted the French flag, and made like we were busy until a tugboat approached, and a guy called Pepe Quero came out, having been expressly sent by Commander Jauregui to find out the name of our Captain, where we came from, etc., etc. and to arrest us if we were the crew of the *Hero*, which they were expecting. But since they didn't recognize our ship, and I had repainted the hull a different color, I told them in poor Spanish, pretending to be a foreigner, that our ship was the *Elizabeth of Burgeos*, that our captain was sick in the cabin and named Garnier and that we came from Veracruz (our ship only had half a load), to pick up a shipment of lumber here if it was ready. That I was the pilot and we would enter the port on the next day, if the principal of the ship so ordered me.

As they waited for me to pay my merchant's fee, and as I surreptitiously negotiated my intention to do business, some of the men from the tugboat were telling me about this guy Cuadra who had escaped from the wharf at Tuspam with the schooner *Hero*, having left its Captain imprisoned, and that they had been ordered to place him under arrest if he arrived in Tampico and to confiscate his cargo since it came from a foreign land. And ready to do so were two platoons waiting on shore, since a certain Colombian Corsaire had warned that the *Hero* would be arriving to port at any moment if the Corsaire didn't catch it out at sea, which it was looking to do.

Taking this into account, my first thought was to get rid of the cargo with all haste; to avoid that they discover it by chance. I had the cook, who had heard everything, go speak with the crew and agree on a course of action. They had to know that the Colombian pirates could reappear at any time and it was necessary to make a decision to avoid a confrontation.

I've already mentioned the condition of our ship. We lacked food and water, none among us was a real seaman, and even though I had studied some in my early years I didn't remember anything. Lastly, none among us had ever been in New Orleans, which was the natural destination that a Frenchman would be headed to. Nevertheless, it was essential that we decide what to do since there was no middle ground; either we resign to be victims of the perverted Jauregui, for whom our misfortune would be his glory, or we could wait to be captured by the pirates who would dispossess us of our goods and dispose of us. Or, we could throw ourselves back out to sea without reservation, with our eyes blinded as to our course and at the mercy of the heavens and the waves, to search through the terrible elements of the seas the protection and asylum that the land refused us.

Although such disconcerting options only served to augment the uncertainty of our lives, we all instinctively decided for the last choice without a doubt. It was the only one that offered some hope. We made ourselves believe that time would benefit us, and at some point a ship traveling back to the United States would take us to a port. At any rate, the results so far convinced us that we couldn't count on being long-term guests here.

We straightened the bow towards where we wished, with a brisk wind, taking the precaution of fasting without which we would have perished, as we will see, and once we had made it out a-ways, we lost track of time and some of us our sanity, during which we spent twenty days rowing hard but making no headway. A furious southern wind came and put us in a dire situation. I assure you the anguish engulfed us and there were those of us who saw their final moments written above in the sky. The sails and rigging couldn't resist the storm. They were smashed, and we found ourselves forced out to sea, for four or five days, to avoid condemning ourselves.

Once the storm subsided, I thought we were near the island of Cuba, which was very dangerous due to the restrictions there. We kept turning around until we thought we had the right course, having a tough time of it due to the dense sea and constant squalls, so much so that it took fifteen days before we saw land. There was a point where we didn't know where we were, which offered us both the opportunity and likewise the risk that there was no more than four yards to the bottom and not too far from the beach. We worried about running aground, and due to the coming and going, here and there, we spent another twenty days halted.

Having no choice, our dismay started to spread despite trying to stay positive. We'd gone over a month at two crackers and one quart of water per person and we had nothing left but the crumbs that we managed to gather, enough water for another day and no wood left to navigate.

This was the condition we were in when we thought we saw a port. It was without a doubt either Galveston or Barataria. But even though we fired our cannon thirty times, after 48 hours of being visible, nobody came out and we could see nothing. At that point some on board proposed a reconnaissance with the small boat, to see if they found a fort of some kind, but I opposed this as I feared that they would desert and leave the rest of us abandoned. Others wanted us to come ashore and march inland, but again I dissuaded them because of the risk of being caught by indians. And at last, helped by a little bit of ,fire water' that I managed to supply through our cook-translator, who did his job well, they agreed that come life or death we would row back out to sea, all night and the following day to see if we would find another vessel to come to our aid.

It just so happened that with an 8 mile per hour wind, and after thirty hours more or less, following constantly the same pace, as the afternoon began to dusk, we discovered on the horizon another schooner under the lee from whom we requested help by flag and cannon blast. She steered closer to the wind, we came alongside with our sails down, and in the blink of an eye we were within trumpet distance. They shouted that they were the *Satiana* coming from Matamoros, and having told them of our situation, they helped us very generously to whatever we needed, except a pilot as they only had one, according to tradition in that profession. However, they did offer to sail in convoy, which we did, entering the Mississippi two days later through the S.O. pass.

Upon throwing anchor, the head of customs came out at once to see us. And seeing as how we had no cargo and no papers, as it had all remained in Tuspam, he sent us under guard to the customs house. Upon our arrival in New Orleans, which was at a distance of thirty leagues from the entry of the river, our arrival was already known due to telegraph, and among the mass of Spaniards that awaited me there at the pier, I was pleased to hug first my always good friend Don Fernando de la Lastra, who like everyone else, had supposed I was dead.

Not long later, Mr. Glover presented himself, captain of the *Hero*, having been set free, due to the intervention of the American diplomat. He had come to find me and recommended that I consign the goods of Don Simon Cuasllu, a merchant here.

And thus ended a campaign brought about through imprudence and a lack of reflection, continued by fear, and brought to a happy conclusion by Divine Providence. But so that the story be complete and neither the narration nor the events appear unbelievable, nor the circumstances of having navigated American waters for sixty days without our mast breaking, nor the privations of so much time on crackers and water, we should therefore add some things. First, during the voyage the crewmen had had their own goods intended for sale, which represented their life savings, and because of that, them as well as I, we accepted whatever resolution to our troubles no matter how disheartening; second, that without knowing it, we had spent a lot of time in the waters that form the bay of Saint Bernard with the Colorado river, and due to this region being inhabited by savages, and not being a frequented route, it could have very well ended up with our remains lying there with the world not knowing, and thirdly, due to the privations we went through, having weighed myself before embarking on this voyage and once again upon my arrival in New Orleans, the difference was twenty three pounds less.

Despite finding myself rather lifeless, the first couple days I busied myself with disembarking the few goods we had, as per the orders of the original partners. I spoke with various vendors directly regarding my situation and business, I chartered a new ship because the *Hero* was condemned and sold as unfit to sail. I arranged what I needed and immediately after (around July) I sent the new goods to Tampico consigned to Don Jose de la Lastra.

Finally having completed this business, I didn't have much of a choice but to stay in New Orleans, as there was no way I could appear in Tampico at the head of the return expedition. Also, during my absence, the conspiracy of Padre Arenas was discovered in Mexico, in which the wicked Jauregui accused me of being complicit, and many had died at the gallows, the same friar, General Arana, and a whole lot of others. But I can swear that I had nothing to do with that, and that during my stay in the country I had no other occupation but earning a fortune to return to my dear homeland. In reality, what Jauregui was looking for was to confiscate my ship and its cargo and the satisfaction of putting me, the man who had fooled him previously, before a firing squad.

Upon ending the business, each partner received his share and therefore, I believed, all would recognize without a fuss the obligation to compensate me for my services that I had rendered. I made sure to stress it to Sr. Lastra as well as others and they, who had other intentions, assured me of my compensation until the moment that they had theirs, and afterwards, they reneged on their word, taking advantage of my absence in Mexico. There was more still; so that nothing would lack from this perfidy, Don Juan de Juncal, with whom I had pooled together funds, took 2,718 silver nickels which belonged to me (less 282 which was my share of the losses), and even though I must have written him a hundred times, that I was sick as a result of the labor and privations of the voyage; even though I belabored the dictionary for words to beg and make him recognize a duty that honor and conscience should dictate - yet when he responded, it was to tell me to find an occupation so I could survive on my own.

I don't know if Juncal conceived of the miserable idea of keeping what was mine at that moment. What I can tell you is that he employed the most shameful means of doing so; regardless of my diligence in taking care of our business and resorting to all kinds of unimaginable things to make a profit. I did not get what was mine until August of 1837, ten years later, when he was ordered to indemnify me my sum by an arbiter we had agreed on.

Fortunately, when I arrived in New Orleans, the eminent, generous and good countryman Don Simon Cuenllu, originally from Mandaca, took me into his house. And I say fortunately, because without his hospitality, and my lack of health, with no economic means at all and in a country whose language I did not know, I would have seen myself irremissibly leading a precarious existence. I collaborated with him with what I could, and during my free time I studied French, I soon found myself able to make it on my own.

My first resolution was to write to Don Jose de la Lastra asking to borrow 1,000 nickels, which he sent me right away. With them and the support of Sr. Cuenllu, I took my first step, building a grocery store of quite high quality; and I began to work again, from dawn until midnight to repair what my adversity and weakness had damaged.

Thus established, it suffices to say that the results reversed not only my previous misfortunes, but after a year I had acquired excellent credit with my vendors. Even to the point of taking whatever I wished from their warehouses to fill my shop, discounting my rate at the banks, like a capitalist.

In March of that year I visited the establishment on the Dauphine street with my friend Mr. Jones. The regulars had an apetite for rums from Cuba and I was rather popular there due to my ability to procure this product. After months of diligence in acquiring each other's maternal languages, I could converse almost fluently with my friend and our chats often carried over to the mornings. We shouted to each other our opinions on life and love and our dreams, trying to be heard over the musicians, including a Spanish guitarist, passing a bottle back and forth, drinking as the other spoke. I was twenty three years old at the time, not having accomplished any of the goals I had set for myself. My eyes kept drifting to an American girl and his attention to one of the dancers. I shared with her my journeys and she spoke of hers, I found her well studied and very pleasant; that night I will never forget.

Not long afterwards, I found myself enjoying my greatest auspices when the expulsion of Spaniards from Mexico occurred. It was surely an act of ingratitude without equal in history, as no son had ever thus demeaned the sacrifices of his parents. Though for me, it became a factor in my prosperity as it multiplied my profits immensly. Young, old, women and children, rich and poor, men of means and the most humble, all piled together and driven off, in not much better conditions than the blacks from Africa, all to New Orleans. Mercilessly thrown out of their own dwellings by their own kin; by those who owed them their own existence, their religion, their culture, customs, the names that they carried, and even the skin color that made them often vain. And everyone instinctively came to me, to find them accommodation, to act as an interpreter, to help with difficulties both personal and peculiar, with the only benefit to me being their consumption in my store. But as it was highly regarded, and the number of outcasts at that time large, and the vast majority had metal with which to pay, and as among them were many ordinary men and I was there to exploit the situation. I built a boarding house, an inn (with billiards), a tavern, and all kinds of games; including *Faraon*, *Buleta*, and *Monte*; and as all these took place during both day and night, and as idleness is the mother of all deviations among men, in very little time I had amassed over 10,000 nickels.

Meanwhile, in the port of Havana, a war expedition was being readied against the Republic of Mexico, commanded by General Barradas, who became famous, despite the blunders of his campaign. It was said at the time that when he insisted on attacking, the authorities in Cuba resisted many times, and at last the influence of ignorance had triumphed as well as the perversity that dominated their courts. Be that as it may, the reality is that three thousand men gathered on those ships, some local and some foreign, and they made off to sea in a convoy headed by a man-of-war and other battle ships, at the command of the arrogant Admiral Laborda. It was known that the squadron left without many of the precautions typical of such a venture; such as they didn't even have Spanish retreat specialists on their ships, to avoid total confusion, nor was there a rally point designated in case of a rout, and due to this unpardonable carelessness, the American frigate *Golconda* was able to detach itself from the fleet with five hundred men, having made the captain, a pure land soldier and always seasick, believe that they had just saved themselves from certain danger; surely as they left the port they were bought and paid by the Republicans to do what they did. And on top of that disaster, instead of taking their soldiers to the breakwater of Tampico or near it, something which would have been convenient for those familiar with the area, the landing occurred at Punto de Jerez and Cabo Rojo, twelve leagues away from Tampico, ushering in the utter disgraceful catastrophe of which we will deal with later.

Let's leave the crown's soldiers jumping on shore, at Punta Jerez, for a moment and let's follow the sail of that lost ship which arrived in New Orleans feigning it had experienced thunderstorms and troubles without end. The troops quartered themselves in a building commandeered by the Governor of the region, and the consul was sent to notify the Spanish authorities in Cuba seeing that, having passed a certain amount of time, the very same General Laborda showed up at the port, with the *Asia*, the *Restauracion*, and the *Cautivo*, to take them to their destination.

The circumstances should've advised Laborda to reembark his troops and lead them without delay to the position of Berradas on the Mexican coasts. But the General, deceived by the incense, festivities and feasts that the indigenous of New Orleans always reveled in, he forgot his obligations, and he didn't depart until forty days had passed.

Among the refugees, the invasion engendered enthusiasm. There were many who took up arms to join the expedition. But I, not a part of them, saw myself later being drawn by the benefits that a daring speculator might find in the new conquests and, more than anything, by the recommendations of certain persons who awarded me the task of provisioning of the army. I sold my store, and taking a good profit from the condition I left it in, I put forth the funds to purchase foods, and I headed on a ship to Tampico with some other civilians, who were all being driven by bad luck as was I, along the path of pleasant delusions.

While we sail our boats to their destination, without notable trouble, let's return to Cabo Rojo to reconnect with the events that play a part in our story: the poor soldiers of Corona, with their chief out front, jumped out onto the hot sand of the beaches, in the dead heat of summer, underneath one of those suns that seems to envelope nature, on one of those scalding hot days that baked the rocks, in which the white hot fierce air one breathes in like bonfires, the poor soldiers of the regiment of Corona, I repeat, marched along the coast, burdened by the weight of their weapons, their equipment and munitions. In that desert, there were no mules available, nor any more water to drink than the brackish water you find when digging a hole near the ocean. And after going through a skirmish at the place called Los Conchos, they arrived at the breakwater, and found the abandoned fort and all the canons destroyed.

From the beachhead they marched on Tampico, and overcoming the small obstacles that the defenders had put in their way, they took over the plaza, they drove off Garza de Altamira, despite the fact that he commanded three times the troops, and finally, upon returning from one of the many inland expeditions during which they were always victorious, they came out victorious, capturing Santa Anna with his entire division, during his attack on the small guard in the city.

With control of Santa Anna, who was by then the most famous general of the Republic, Barranda would've undoubtedly made his own name famous by sending the Mexican general to Havana. But the imbecile let himself be deceived during a conference the two of them had. Santa Anna made him believe that the independence of Mexico was impossible to satisfy the people, and that he was resolved to support the intentions of Spain, that Mexico ought to submit itself to her domination once again. That in this sentiment he had the support of the Republican army, and that he hoped to be let free to realize his plan, which would occur at once. The Spanish general, more honorable than intelligent, believed in this fraud. He ignored whom he was dealing with, someone not known for justice or decorum, who was rather well known for his immorality and fallaciousness. And not only did he allow him to return with his troops to Pueblo Viejo, on the other side of the river, but there are actually people who swear that he supported him monetarily, which the traitor Santa Anna said he required.

The moment Santa Anna found himself free, he ordered Barrandas to surrender, via a taunting communique that would've embarassed even a field sergeant. At that point ensued extraordinary times, in which the locals flooded the barracks and the warehouses, with a loss of the majority of my goods, completely halting my operations. And while an attack would've defeated our enemy, who was completely disorganized, the consequences of the absurd landing at Punta de Jerez and Cabo Rojo made impossible any assault as that horrible heat, the brackish water, the unbelievable exhaustion, the humidity and the privations, drove to the hospitals four-fifths of the Spanish forces, leaving behind to defend the city less than five hundred men.

The presence of such a disconcerting scene bewildered the General, who feared being left without a single healthy man, since the scurvy and fevers were wreaking havoc, and that's the only way that one can explain the capitulation, in which their arms were lowered and flags turned over, without having lost a single battle. But the most unheard of part of it was not the surrender of our army nor the joy with which the Mexicans hung up the Spanish standard in their Congress notwithstanding having been battered and humiliated during each encounter on the field, rather that the capitulation was not understood, not by those who accompanied the division as volunteers, nor the speculators, nor that battalion that had gone missing in the *Golanda*, since nobody even remembered them.

Santa Anna, with his court, took control of Tampico. And the unpunished murder of several innocents was the first sign of the kind of protection and security that was in store for those who'd surrendered. The infamy did not stop at that: during a banquet that same day, the federales were celebrating their glorious triumph, they agreed to a surprise attack on the detachment at the small fort of la Barra, which had not heard of the surrender having been without communication for some time now. And drunk with pleasure at the thought of finally being victorious over the castilian army, even though their success was due to vile treachery, a thousand men volunteered, and those officers who had distinguished themselves so well in the saloons and the bars due to their shyness of confronting the sons of Spain now placed themselves at the forefront of this expedition, flushed due to my whiskey being doled about at that time.

The fortress was impetuously attacked in the dark, and although the guard held one hundred and fifty valients, much of them sick with fever, including Colonel Vazquez who commanded, they resisted fearlessly several different assaults, and the fields already covered and the ditches filled with more than five hundred cadavers, among them almost all of the authors of this criminal enterprise, the pressured defenders of the fort were not content with heroically stopping the aggression, but they then went on the offensive, they abandoned their trenches upon hearing the voice of their commander Vizarro, who didn't quit fighting even when pegged by a bullet, and charged by bayonet over the enemy survivors, they chased them a great distance, abandoning them at last to their appropriate ignominy where history would castigate them.

Having been skewered, just as they had planned on skewering ours, they told our men of the capitulation, and after an official had gone to make certain of this, they accepted the surrender on the condition that they not turn over their arms until the moment they vacated the territory. The battalion from New Orleans arrived at the scene of the catastrophe after these events had occurred. Barradas sought refuge in the United States, only to die later on in Paris of his own misery. And I never received word that the government in Madrid ever sought to punish him in any way, those whose failed methods precipitated the calamity of the venture which should've had good results for Spain. Not because I think the conquest of the Republic an easy task, rather that the victory of Tailor at the head of an undisciplined mob has come to demonstrate evidently what our soldiers should've been capable of, being commanded by Arredondo or by another experienced soldier, who knew the terrain and the customs of the natives.

Immediately after having consummated this tragedy over the Tamaulipas war, which we have covered since my own personal fortunes were involved, the boat in which I was on and the ones who headed the retreat stopped in Tampico, and we all knew with surprise and heartache the lamentable state of our compatriots. We stayed a few days at the breakwater watching over the embarkment of the troops, and having finished this operation, we set off to Havana, where we arrived dismantled due to a fierce storm which caused substantial damage among the warships.

Since it was natural after two months of hardship, after disembarking my goods, a good portion of them were in bad shape. And thus it was just able to satisfy an indemnification that could not be covered, even though what was left we sold fairly well, in a public auction, it was barely enough to cover the costs and the freightage.

Fortunately, the man who had purchased my establishment in New Orleans still owed me two thousand silver nickels, without which this would be the third time that I would find myself penniless. I marched there, and it turns out that during this tragic period, my purchaser had passed away and his widow had no interest in business, I decided to take it over once again. We came to an agreement, and I kept the business on very reasonable conditions, and above all else without having to pay a premium.

I renewed my connection with Mr. Jones and the community of merchants, managing to recuperate everything I had lost through diligence and dedication, despite the circumstances not being the same now that Spaniards were allowed reentry in the Republic and the amount of consumers fell. I sold my business again and headed to Tampico where my brother Jose was living, young and full of the hope of what his great abilities had in store, especially notable was his seriousness and moderation, and very notable as he spoke and wrote English and French with the same perfection as Castilian, thanks to having attended an American college in Kentucky for two years, paid for by me, I forgot to mention.

The welcome I received in Tampico when I arrived was the best. Those who had returned earlier and who knew me had taken it upon themselves to speak of me very highly and placed a halo on my reputation which, according to them, was merited due to my services in New Orleans. Then, just as I had decided, I started the best grocery store that existed there during that era, I brought my brother with me, and I worked without wasting any time at all, my prosperity continually growing, until an unexpected event cut short the rapid return of my fortune.

Near the end of 1832 or early 1833, the so called liberals staged a *coup* in the area of Tamaulipas. And this name, liberal, has been usurped by so many, here and in other places, by those who wanted to take control of public institutions to live at the expense of others; they took advantage of the innocence of the townsfolk to present themselves as supreme patriots, and came to power under the pretense of abolishing taxes and tariffs (which never came about), and dragged the rest of us into ruin and loss.

The incendiary revolution quickly spread to our place, as it was always the first task of any rebellion to take over a port with which to import foreign goods without tariffs to finance their activities. And a stubborn man named Tomas Rosell, son of Campeche although a cataluñan native, who never ceased to gloss over his own iniquities in the name of patriotism, having later made himself the leader of the insurgents, he soberly decreed that all Spaniards were to be expelled, giving them eight days to arrange their belongings.

Such arbitrary action made the victim's situation all the more dangerous, as there were now fewer people one could trust. In such unfortunate situations there was a man who gave his desk to his indigenous dependant, who ended up betraying him, who ended up turning over his store to his wife, who was later tricked as she did not understand anything; who passed on her assets to a local under certain conditions which were never fulfilled, and who took residence with a native godson of hers, who owed her everything, and upon the husband's return found his house burnt to the ground. Don Jose de la Lastra had left his wealth and turned over his businesses to an Italian named Avesana who threw everything out the window, bringing his benefactor in disgrace and later ruin. I sold what I had to a Veracruzano, who offered me no guarantees of its return except his word, on the condition that I pay him five hundred nickels monthly, and my brother, who at the insistence of a lady of influence was spared from exile, would not have been able to take over my operations. And it pained me again as I was certain that this would be the fourth time that I would be wounded again with misfortune.

Forced thus by threats to abandon our businesses and relationships, and not having anything but the brigantine *Aguascalientes*, dischartered through age, we had no choice but to embark on this condemned ship, because neither reason nor begging were enough for them to allow us time for other ships. This travesty plaid out as you can imagine. We arrived, by miracle, in New Orleans, after quite a while of navigating the seasonal weather and taking turns on the pump to keep ourselves from sinking.

Our stay in the capital of Louisiana had no other purpose than to wait out the events that had caused our departure. Therefore everybody was under the illusion that we would spend a few days here and return to our houses one day. I, a fan of music and playing the flute quite well, joined a group of other youngsters who plaid various instruments, and formed a little band which gave us a pleasurable and honest occupation, and which served as the center of a crowded and pleasant society. But bad luck sought me out the more fun I had; I started to spurt blood from my mouth with such abundance and frequency that two groups of accredited doctors whom I consulted were of the opinion that some mortal accident had befallen me, as they imagined the spilling had to do with this or that organ (it ended up being a stomach ulcer).

Despite this, it didn't affect me in the slightest, as I felt no pain or inconvenience of any kind. More so since the flow of blood never decreased in spite of all the treatments, and I resolved to return to Spain, not without first obtaining a wooden branch called Anacahuita by the indians, which is reputed by them to be a cure for hemorrhages of all types.

This admirable remedy, which consists of drinking at all hours of the day the concoction prepared from the juice of the wood of said tree, boiling its splinters in clean water until the volume fell by half, and I drank it which served to make me completely healthy after eight days of using it. I never again suffered anything similar in the twenty seven years since then to this day where I write these lines. And I'm also convinced, after having recommended this to numerous patients with success, that medical science is nothing more than a trick of quackery paid for by ignorance.

What's undoubtable is that it's been over two thousand years since people have been complaining that the language of medicine is indecipherable to the sick; that health always finds a thousand reefs to collide on; that various treatments, both good and bad, are sold for fortunes of gold, that all health systems have to first be exaggerated, and then demolished by its very own practice, and lastly, that a simple diploma, unmerited at times, concedes the right to doctors to destroy everything without heeding to anyone; the law protecting them from the imprudence of a prescription that could drive someone who takes it straight to the grave. And even today we know that no government nor nation has regulated the medical field, also ridiculous. Although supported by the law of the highest social need, it has not organized itself to the same level as other fields, as the hierarchy in medicine does not guarantee the acts of any of its members.

The indians employ to this day in their medicines the same methods used by the two famous doctors of antiquity, Chiron and Esculapio. Experience is their only guide, as was for those two great men of medicine. And, according to the opinion of an eminent professor, the benefits of medicine began to diminish since Hipocrates introduced his oaths. Because fiction took the place of simplicity, and his contradictory theories paved the way for the homicidal and diabolic inventions that decimate civilized society.

In the year 1832, taking advantage of the fact that two friends were going to Europe, as business called them to England, I partnered with them, leaving my revitalized store in the capable hands of my brother Jose. We decided to make the trip by land to New York, uniting the fun and brief with certainty and comfort, and around September, for forty nickels, which included room and board, we began our journey on the steamer *Peruvian*, towards Louisville, a distance of 1,450 miles from New Orleans.

We navigated upstream at six knots, despite the current being another six and the depth being no more than forty fathoms in front of the city, and in the first days passing by a beautiful countryside covered by estates and immense plantations, we arrived at Baton Rouge, a city which occupies the sunny hillside of the first elevation you find during the trip.

Otherwise the terrain is completely flat and quite marshy, inhabited for the most part by French and Spaniards.

Continuing on our course, we came to the mouth of the Colorado river, sometimes called the Red river, which bathes this immense country with the finest cotton, and which abundantly produces sugar, maiz and other fruits. This river is the last tributary of the Mississippi and its length is so considerable that its origin is in the Sierra de Tatos, forty leagues further than Santa Fe of New Mexico, and passes through different tribes who do much commerce through its waterways.

From here, the Mississippi extends in a series of lateral canals called Bayoux, which disperses the water during the flooding of the plains. Without them, not being able to divert the water towards the Gulf of Mexico and Lake Pontchartrain and Mobile, the magnificent estates of Louisiana, including New Orleans herself, would find themselves flooded on a regular basis. When the plains flood, the water level rises as much as forty feet.

The Mississippi river serves as a border for the state of Louisiana, which owes its name to having been discovered by the French during the reign of Luis XIV. The western part, with New Orleans, was ceded to Spain in 1773 via a secret treaty, to indemnify the many sacrifices it had made in 1761. Some years later, in 1801, without a doubt due to the one of the scoundrels from our government at the time, it was ceded to Napoleon. But when that colossus attempted to begin various grand projects there, a war broke out which led to the Peace of Amiens, and he ended up selling it to the Americans.

The main city of this state, New Orleans, was founded around 1718 or 1719 by the government of Bienville and his men, since an extraordinary storm had obligated them to establish themselves in the area, as the bay of Mobile, in which they found themselves, had been filled with sand. It's situated about 90 miles from Belize, which is one of the main points of entry into the Gulf of Mexico.

Its first inhabitants gave it the name which still stands, to perpetuate the legacy of Philip of Orleans. But despite all the efforts of the West India Company, to whom several tax exemptions were afforded in order to develop and colonize that land, they nevertheless experienced a miserable life there. And only when the government of these lands became not just a tyranny over them but an expression of their will, and at times their humble servants, was finally when this city and the state of Louisiana was able to reach the apex of prosperity which it finds itself in. And the best thinkers today, see the day not far when New Orleans will become the most frequented port in the entire United States, despite its unhealthy climate.

Five or six miles below the city, between the estates named Rodriguez and Bienvenida, is the site where the Americans defeated the British on the 8th of January, 1815. With just five or six thousand men haphazardly formed, they defeated the twelve thousand commanded by General Packenham of Wellington's army, who paid with his life for the audacity of underestimating his enemy.

General Jakson, captain of the Republicans, displaid in those moments a certain valor, a firmness and an energy without which it would have been impossible to overcome the obstacles faced by his troops. He imposed martial law, and imprisoned a judge who invoked habeas-corpus for a member of the legislature who had protested against various measures taken by the general. Most admirable was, having reestablished law and order, the magistrate condemned the general, imposing a fine of 1,000 nickels for his breach of law- and it is no less extraordinary that he paid it as a civilian regardless of the traditional military tribunals.

In the city there are numerous spacious roads, uniform plazas, and a series of notable public buildings, in neighborhoods which to this day contain inscriptions dating back to the time of the Spanish government. The paving is good and the brickwork is about 6 feet wide. Temples are to be seen everywhere and of every denomination, since all are free to worship as they please. But The Cathedral, which is the most important, is Catholic, since most of the original population were Catholic as well as their descendents; and I met and did business with the famous Capuchino Fray Antonio de Sedella, a Cordovian, who died as parish priest at ninety some years of age after having started as the garrison chaplain in the town established by the Viceroy of New Spain, around the year '70.

Father Antonio, which is how everyone called him, never gave up the habits, the long beard, and the sandals of his religion, even though later on it was no longer customary. With his exceptional dress, he went gray dedicating his life to doing good, and though he never made Bishop, he was considered the patriarch of the religion in that city, and as the founder of the churches that exist for the Christian faith.

Upon his death his body was on public display for three days. During those days, masses of people without distinction came to kiss his feet and shed a tear over his coffin as a final goodbye. And furthermore, I saw his robe being divided into thousands of tiny pieces to be distributed among the faithful, as no one wanted to be left without a memory of him, or better said, no one wanted to be left without a true relic. The three days having transpired, the Orleanseans suggested that the body pass through the city's main avenues, and thus it was, accomanied by a great crowd, the Spaniards acting as pall bearers. It's impossible to describe what happened. The laments and tears produced a despondency so pervasive, and people hovered over the balconies and windows, seeing the inanimate body pass by, the profusion of flowers and laurel wreathes made it look like judgment day.

While this occurred, the local statesmen gathered, composed of men of all sects, and they repealed the law that prohibited one from being buried in a church, and father Antonio was sepulchered in the one he presided over. Everybody attended his service, including the major businesses and all centers of commerce and government were closed. And when the remains of this man, loved by all, lay entombed in the pantheon built for this purpose, the legislators convened again and reinstated the law which they had just suspended.

As for the people, Creoles are by and large refined and friendly, and they treat strangers with open arms, especially Spaniards, of whom they have good memories. As proof of this, I am pleased to write to you what Mr. Flint wrote in his geography „Whatever the reason may be, the yolk of the Spanish government was always easy and light upon the anglo-Americans that lived under it. And even to this day, the time when they ruled here is spoken of as the ‚Golden century'."

Having now paid the debt of gratitude I owed to the town that took me in at my most vulnerable, precisely when it looked like I would lose my entire fortune, let's continue the description of my travels, if only to note the peculiarities that we came upon in transit, which don't seem odd to me now as I relate to you my life story.

Continuing our pilgrimage, we entered Natchez, which is a beautiful villa built on a little hill which overlooks the eastern bank of the Mississipi, it was founded by the franciscans who constructed there Fort Rosalia, giving it the name it now bares, as that is the name of the savages living around that territory. But such were the humiliations that they inflicted on the poor indians, by the commander and the officers of the stronghold, that the natives resolved to take revenge. Too weak themselves to realize their intentions, they convened with other tribes bordering themselves to behead each and every one of their oppressors. Having no almanac to divine at which time they should complete the general dismemberment, the tribes compromised by planting fifteen stakes in each of their respective fields, of which they would yank out one each day. On the day the last stake was removed, a large number of the conquistadors had their heads removed within the hour. The surviving indians avenged the deaths of their brothers, destroying the recently founded city, which would not be rebuilt for many years.

A few hours after passing the mouth of the Arkansas river, lying about 191 miles from New Orleans, we came upon a hut hidden away in the woods which indicated the sad conditions of its inhabitants, and walking briefly around the vicinity, while the boatman replenished his provisions of wood, we came across a stone on a gravesite, next to the house, rustically adorned, with the following inscription:

"Here lies Jean Randolf, who was tossed into the river along this beach. Having found in his pockets a sum of 1,353 *pesos* in bank notes, we advise his family or he who believes it is his right, and with justification, to introduce himself to recover these." Immediately we headed to the door to see if such an act of integrity had been followed through, and a right old man greeted us, who even after having put notice of the death in the newspapers of neighboring states, even to that day still held the money, as nobody had come to reclaim it.

Admiring such integrity that has few peers, we boarded again our vessel and continued our journey, reaching a town of little importance named New Madrid. Without a doubt the name of the town got our attention, and coming into town inquisitively, we crossed paths with a Jesuit, who told us that the town was founded by Spaniards who still comprised the majority of residents, and who in 1812 survived an earthquake whose likes had never been seen which resulted in the river coming out of its banks, submerging the town and leaving no survivors among those who stayed.

Seventy four miles from this town, Madrid, you find the confluence of the Mississippi and Ohio rivers. And such is the violence with which these two powerful rivals crash that it offers the spectacular sight of having their courses nearly paralyzed for almost twenty miles before they meet.

From the confluence of these two rivers, which I'll say is about two thousand miles from New Orleans, we navigated up the Ohio and arrived at Paduca, where it joins the Tenesi river. There we noticed that many women were smoking pipes. From there we went to Potosi, from Potosi to Palmira, Troya, Rome and Carthage, to arrive finally at Albani, where we had to disembark as at the point the river rapids were too strong to navigate. In carriage then, we arrived in Louisville which is an important town serving as the key to the rest of Kentucky. By the way, at a certain distance from this city, which at the start of the century was nothing more than an observation post built by General Clark, is the town of Bardstown, inside which, in a Jesuit school, my unforgettable brother was educated.

In the state of Kentucky there are a great number of Yankees that have migrated from the western part of New York and Connecticut. They are like the Galicians of the United States. When they leave the house of their parents, they receive nothing more than a chair to sit on, a yoke of oxen, an axe and pickaxe. With just these tools they cross three, maybe four thousand miles, before definitively settling down. Afterwards, in general, they no longer hear word from their parents, nor their parents from them.

Cincinati, which we came upon right away, is a city which from the outset began to show signs of the grandness it is known for. Although Columbus is the capital of the state, Cincinati is the most populous, the most prosperous, the most commercial and most industrial. And due to her great agricultural productivity she has come to deserve the distinguished name of "Queen of the West."

The Ohio reaches all the way to Pittsburg where either the ice or the extraordinary shallowness of the waters create impediments to our traversing. Coming across the second of these two, we had to begrudgingly renounce our travel via waterway, it being more comfortable, fun, and safer, and also shortening the distance required, and cheaper, in favor of taking a seat in a cramped and dangerous carriage. We gathered our luggage, including a container of Chacolique (light wine from the Bascongadas) which had been sent to me by my father shortly before we left New Orleans, and we continued on our path.

Four powerful horses, driven by a half-crazed conductor, that we had to swap out every hour, were in charge of taking us at breakneck speed on a poorly built road. We hit so many bumps and knocking into one another, that it produced a fatal movement, at some point during the day a reign snapped off from the vehicle, and in the pitch black of night we were shook so hard that one of the crossbeams broke loose and our carriage ran off the road. Several of us were injured and knocked unconscious. Among them were my companions Palacio (Don Manuel) and Don Joaquin de Errazu, leaving me with the most minimal of injuries and thankfully the container of wine unharmed.

As a consequence of this stumble we had to walk a whole league on foot, until we reached the first hamlet where they helped us rehabilitate our carriage and we were able to reach a town called Xenia. There they built us a new one, and we were able to ride out the storm, passing by Colombus the capital of Ohio, which communicates with New York via Lake Erie and counts among its towns Urbanam, Medina, Cadiz, Union and Batabia - we gladly arrived at Weeling which belongs to the state of Virginia and bordered by Pennsylvania.

A short distance from Wheeling, the island of Blamerkasset grabs the attention of travelers due to its three mild length, it's beautiful fertility, and for the memory of a catastrophe which gave it its name.

An Irish gentleman, fleeing from the horrors of the revolution that engulfed his homeland in 1801 and finding refuge in America, came to this island with his entire family. Rich and a lover of beauty, he converted it into a sort of paradise which he enjoyed until 1810 when a horrific fire buried his only daughter under the ruins of the magnificent palace he had built there as his residence. And having abandoned the place of such pain, he became involved in a conspiracy whose objective was to destroy the Union of the States, having to flee at last back to Europe.

We left Weeling through a rather difficult and dangerous route. We crossed the Allegheny mountains, which has an abundance of oats, and we gladly observed an infinite amount of walnut, oak, chestnut, fern, fruit bearing trees and other plants that we had not seen since we had left Spain. And crossing a fertile country side, whose condition we found extraordinary, including the home of Jefferson, we arrived safe yet weary at the capital of the Republic.

In Washington City, all of my anxiety about going to New York and from there embark on to Europe was directed toward revalidating my status as an American citizen, which, according to the law, I had acquired during my residence in the country.

My time in the capital reintroduced to me the perversions that accompany democracy in what were called political machines and the growing antagonism between the so-called Northern and Southern states, which I have avoided til now, and of which I will have much to say later on. I had the misfortune of dining with men who described themselves as entrepreneurs but whose efforts were spent in the halls of the legislature securing contracts to manufacture weapons and for the construction of various public works. Their fortunes being tied directly to the escalation of conflict, they described the efforts to expel westward all Indians with the justification of making the land safe for Christians. These endeavors were to be funded from tariffs on trade and the issuance of debts, burdens to be paid by all citizens.

How these men could describe themselves as Christians nor be tormented by their conscience, remains a mystery. Their goal to see all Indians dead or displaced for their own profits should have sickened any decent man. Even with their own countrymen, the South Carolinians, who had resisted efforts to impose further tariffs on themselves for what they saw as private gains, these men were willing to settle the issue with bloodshed. I found these views to be held by a great number of individuals in the capital, and although they held positions of rank in the republic, they would not be considered gentlemen anywhere else in the country.

Not wishing to remain in Washington any longer than necessary, we concluded our business and made our way north. After Maryland we crossed again into Pennsylvania, which leads to the state of New Jersi. Here I was impressed by the amount of activity and in particular the construction of a rail line for a locomotive, the first one I had seen. But I could not have imagined what awaited me in the city of New York, nor could anything I had previously lived through have prepared me. We took a steamship to the island of Manhattan, and came into a sea of humanity that had little resemblance to the rest of the country. I had the impression most New Yorkers were foreigners, and even those who had been born in the city carried themselves differently. There was a desire among its inhabitants to excel at industry, an ambition that had always spoken to me and which I understood very well. I had the inclination to stay, and seek my fortune here, for the fervor of its people was contagious. There were ships disembarking which brought people and goods of all sorts, while others left for foreign lands; clearly commerce reigned here. I likely would've made this city my own, but I had committed myself to my colleagues in a joint venture and I would not so quickly break my word.

Our goods, which we purchased through brokers consisted of cotton, tobacco, sugar, molasses, and hemp. The English at the time had a limitless appetite for American crops, and there were regular shipments to London, with the return leg of the voyage normally bringing luxurious goods from Europe. My colleagues nominated me as the negotiator once we arrived in London, and although the merchants were keen to do business, there were many other Americans offering similar goods. At last we were able to unload our goods at a reasonable price, especially the Virginia tobacco which sold at a premium, and purchased goods for our return. I did not desire to stay in London any longer than necessary. However, Don Joaquin and Don Palacio, unable to resist the urge of visiting their families with their fatherland so close, made a detour to Spain. I was far too restless thinking of the state of my affairs. Within a week I found myself again on the waves of the Atlantic, reliving that journey as an adult I had made as a child so long ago.

Though not as profitable as I had envisioned, the travels were exciting since I had seen much of the country that provided me with the means to make my fortune. Not only that, but during the passage I befriended an American of English ancestry, Mr. Hardenbrook, who lived in New York. I refrained from returning to New Orleans and spent some time in that magnificent city. Mr. Hardenbrook was occupied in raising funds for large investments in property and commerce. These projects involved construction of rail lines to carry locomotive trains, all the way from New York to Baltimore and another as far as Ohio. The sums of money that these men dealt in were far beyond what I was accustomed. I made my way to the New York Stock & Exchange located on the Wall street in Manhattan, where shares of any enterprise could be bought or sold, and where debts of anyone could be likewise exchanged. I imagined myself making my fortune in this world, though in the end, not even New York could satisfy my hunger; something much stronger kept pulling at me.

Upon returning to New Orleans, months having passed, I was pleased to find my brother maintaining the grocery; the truth is he better managed my own business than I ever did. In retrospect one should not have been surprised, given his intelligence and ease with languages, but nonetheless I was immensely proud of him. Jose had even put to use my own capital, without my permission, in order to speculate in cotton contracts, although after seeing the profits I quickly forgave him. The store functioning with no effort on my part, it became obvious that my time and efforts should be focused in another direction.

What had not changed was the struggle between the territories and the mother country. The urge to rebel against the crown, in fact, seemed to be growing and it was simply a matter of time before the revolution which had created the Mexican Republic would spread further into the Caribbean. Considering that this phenomena had on multiple occasions brought the ruination of my fortune, and death to many others, for no other crime than being born a Spaniard, I did not hold the most sympathetic feelings towards the *independistas*.

But experience taught me many things; that among turmoil comes opportunities for those living with open eyes. And it was easy to see then that the people of New Orleans, and Americans everywhere, had a great appetite for liquors of all kinds, especially *aguardientes* and the potent rums of the islands. I happily set myself to the task of satisfying this thirst, quietly chartered a ship, *La Bella,* and sought out a crew.

Fortunately, for my purposes, at the time there were a great number of refugees from Cuba with native knowledge of the islands, and I took great care in the choices for my employees. We made our way to Havana, bearing a U.S. flag into port and taking care to avoid any ships belonging to the Republic of Mexico; they could very well still have orders for my arrest. Having reached land, I began intensely negotiating to procure the best rum on the island intent on paying the most favorable price. I had my accomplice, Ignacio Morer, a young local I hired in New Orleans, approach each vendor after I had done so in order to secure another price quote. Without realizing Ignacio was in my employ, nor that the goods were destined for the wealthy United States, the boy filled our ship to the brim with bottles at such a discount to what I had initially expected that I didn't hesitate to invite the crew to a feast in the city before returning.

Merchants in New Orleans lined up to buy from me, and I had no problems in selling all of the goods. I made three similar trips that year, and I bought a second ship which I named *La Hermosa* and each round trip brought much the same results. My reputation at the time reached far and expert navigators left other ventures to work for me. Agents from as far as Charleston placed orders in advance with me. The other rum runners must have been confused, or so I heard, by how much I could undercut their most competitive offers, not knowing the secrets to my success.

But as every journey comes to an end, just as every wave rises and breaks, a great tragedy struck that took the wind out of my sails, the loss so great that humanity itself would be disadvantaged. Don Simon Cuenllu and a priest arrived at my home in February early one morning and informed me that my brother had died. They took me to his apartment and showed me the body of Jose, having taken his own life by hanging. His eyes were closed, a white sheet covered him.

Don Cuenllu spent the day with me preparing the funeral, and I later wrote a letter to our parents and agonized over the words. Nothing I could put to paper would convey my utter agony, nor soften the anguish that I knew would echo from their hearts. A great number of visitors came by, keeping me company for several days and bringing me gifts. When I managed to sleep I had dreams of my brother. I saw the two of us swimming in the sea where we came from. One of the gifts left for me sat upright on the table, in brown glass, which I reached for to fight the insomnia. I found myself seeking that warmth over and over again, like a spell that falls on young lovers.

I repeatedly asked myself, and continue to this day, why he lost the will to live. He had not made it known to me that his heart ached, and when we spent time together I had not detected that he was troubled. But a friend revealed that Jose had become withdrawn during the past year, and spoke at times about an emptiness of purpose, he felt he lacked a purpose. How could I have not noticed in my own brother that things were not what they used to be? After several weeks the duties of the enterprises I had worked to create began to demand my attention again. The partners called on me to return to what I knew how to do best, but I refused them all.

A letter from Spain arrived; my mother writing not knowing yet of what had happened, inquiring as to our health and imploring me to watch over Jose. Without a word, I took the next ship leaving for Havana. The events of the following two years would be best described as *una recorrida por las tiñeblas*. On the other side of this time I emerged having little fortune and even less of a reputation. If you could have seen me in those years you would not have been able to recognize your own father; instead you would see the shell of a possessed man.

By the end of 1834, I had wasted most of my wealth in the bars and brothels of the Cuban capital and resisted the calls of my friend Don Jose de la Lastra to return to New Orleans. As one approaches the lowest level of iniquity and human depravity, there comes a moment when a choice appears to either continue eternally into oblivion and sin; or, to stand up again on one's feet, fighting off the shame, and begin following a path worth living. The damage I had brought to others and myself had left many scars both visible and not, and I vowed to myself one wretched morning to overcome my grief and reposition that lost ship known as Clemente de la Cuadra. It was in my search for renewal that my eyes first landed on Señorita Teresa Lopez Doriga.

After several unsuccessful negotiations with the local barons, including a conversation with Miguel Tacón, whose name would more appropriately be *Tacaño*, I made my way out of the Governor's office when laughing voices, of the feminine sort, grabbed my attention and drew me to the ballroom. I edged the door open and peeked in to the sight of women in their most elegant and glorious dresses as a small orchestra plaid a tune from the corner. A pair of brown eyes caught mine immediately, belonging to a girl of remarkable beauty and refined features, reciprocating the same intensity with which I studied her.

I made my way outside with a group of officers, and asked after the name of this girl, attempting that my inquiry appear casual. But these men were preoccupied with the possibility of an insurrection by the negroes of the island, while my head kept returning to the window of the ballroom. I mounted on my horse to make the trip to the capital, and glanced one last time, and saw her there, feeling a stronger desire than ever in my life to walk back into that house.

The next few days I spent in a daze wandering the piers of Havana, supposedly to meet with wholesalers but really lost and living in my own fantasies, stumbling into others as I walked about, my mind fixed on the sight of her and those eyes and energy. Half of the time I thought it was fruitless and that I should not pursue impossibilities; these were just the dreams of a boy. But a week later I managed to have myself invited on a social night while pretending to be there for business. More than anything in my life I wanted to see her again, but I controlled myself in spite of my haste and spoke convincingly of profitable opportunities to those interested in such things.

I didn't have to wait long, in the interim between discussions she found me in the gardens staring at the full moon. She was as sweet as candy, and after that day I would return frequently and stare at her through the window, and later she wore nothing for me and wore it so well. I have no misgivings about speaking of my feelings for your mother in this way. I had no doubts about what I wanted in life nor did she, and we presented ourselves to her father soon after with a *fait accompli*. I pressed aggressively for her hand and wrote a letter to her father, Don Enrique Lopez, stating the following:

'In Teresita I see great characteristics which I imagine would be necessary to be happy. And I would like for you, as surely you are interested in her having the fortune of many titles, to steadfastly examine my deeds and character, and later to tell me if you consider me worthy of her hand, in which case I would be ready to marry her forthwith.'

Truth be told there was resistance to our desires, though this was understandable because of my recent behavior, but my reputation as a trader had reached even to the rural areas of the island and it was hinted that her family would agree to our marriage on the condition that I enter civil society in a respectable fashion, and be able to provide for her in a reputable manner.

I needed little such motivation to reinvigorate my efforts and began delivering goods again from the Caribbeans to the Americans, as I had experience in doing. You will learn one day when you are of age and meet your girl that the actions you take would ordinarily be thought of as reckless and inappropriate. But when she has her chains tied around you there is little you can do except follow your heart. Like a madman and working like a fury I soon had a venture carrying sugar, molasses and rum to be sold through my partners in New Orleans. Within a year we had our own home in Havana and your mother and I married.

All the other years of my life fade away compared to the joy of those years on the island, but as I've said before life flows along a wave of success and failure, pleasure and agony, between two opposing extremes and the transitions between them. I did not agree with the view of many that negroes were inferior and needed to be subjugated, and I felt a moral imperative to counteract this injustice. There were newsletters dedicated to this subject, written by Jose Antonio Saco and Domingo del Monte, among others, all widely circulated and written in anonymity, which received monetary support from me. When it was requested I did what I could to unite family members who had been sold apart, and I encouraged many who came to me with supplications, to leave Cuba for the friendly shores of Louisiana.

And thus the local officials uncovered what I was doing over the years and began making my business activities more difficult. Although the threats never bothered me, the harassment eventually found my children, and after an incident which turned violent, I decided New Orleans would be safer for my family. My son Enrique inherited many peculiarities from his father, he made a habit of escalating confrontations when it may have been healthier to navigate away from them.

And thus ended a beautiful part of my life through the intolerance of my supposed countrymen; they thought of themselves as giants the moment they stepped out of their own country. I felt a great hatred for these men, especially later when I learned that the responsible individual was a certain Spaniard by the name of O'Donnell who had murdered many negroes to gain favor with the crown. A great weight afflicted my soul, though I had no desire to replicate the effects of my last depression, and so set myself to the task of business, having learned that the remedy to my misery was dedicated labor.

Before long I tired of shipping the vices of others over the seas, not to mention that my competitors had wizened to my methods. Instead I decided to ship their vices across land, buying into a new issue of railway company shares, courtesy of Mr. Hardenbrook. Railroad lines were being laid everywhere it seemed, so much so that one couldn't turn around without seeing a new line being built. New Orleans, being the largest shipping port in the United States, was in my mind a natural destination to which the inhabitants of other cities would seek to connect. The Mississippi Central line brought us into the city of Jakson in Tenesi, which itself connected to lines in Memphis with further tracks to Charleston or north to Cincinati.

Most of my time I spent writing letters, proposals, opinions on the proposals of others, and revising and examining the figures in my ledger book. Contrary to running rum, being a capitalist did not exert the same strains physically, which suited my age, but mentally the adventure was far more dangerous. Together with Don Jose de la Lastra, as well as the sons of Sr. Cuenllu, who had greatly supported me in my early years in New Orleans, and my friend Mr. Jones, from the days of our escape from Tuspam, we partnered together and bought interests in the shares of railroad companies, mills, foundries, hotels, public parks and properties around the city which we took upon ourselves to preserve.

A peculiar coincidence seems to befall individuals who have amassed any amount of wealth in that others seek to relieve them of such a burden..."

And here Don Clemente drops off his pen. Our grandfather leaves us with the aching desire to know the remaining gaps of his amazing life. His memoirs contain no further pages or indications of the following events. From anecdotal stories we know that he was betrayed and cheated by a colleague in New Orleans, though he managed to reverse the fortunes on his enemy, in a less than reputable way. There are whispers of railroad deals, a two year trip to find gold in California, and a lethal encounter with a Mexican warship. We do know that he made it to Spain and continued living in the way we have grown used to reading about. The legendary fortune he described joins him in the town of Utrera, where our family today has its roots, and together with an inheritance from his father, uncle and his wife's inherited wealth, he embarked on the greatest land purchase in the history of Andalucia leaving the Cuadra family with an estate over 5,000 hectares.

What you may not have heard is that Don Clemente made it a personal goal to bring education and modernity to his adopted home of Utrera. He purchased and renovated several lots along the rundown centre, building himself a home adequate for a gentleman of his standing, as well as paying with his own funds for the repavement of the adjacent roadways and a great arch connecting to his neighbors home under which all would pass to reach the city centre. Showing the same vigor in his later years as he had in fighting the waves and bandits in the New World, he entered into the bullring of politics. Seeing clearly the ruinous effect of the interests of the political factions taking precedence over the interests of the community at large, Don Clemente set himself as a candidate in the electoral campaign for mayor.

A liberal mayor faced a constant battle against the influence of the moderates and conservatives in the national government, although Don Clemente was beloved by his neighbors and the townsfolk. He denounced and corrected the vices that the administration he now ran had been perpetrating and at the end of his mandate, to clarify his actions before the public, he wrote and published an account and general ledger of his office and activities, and seeing as how unexpected this was, and clearly stated, it was eagerly read by the public. It was said at the time that, being one of the most respected actions that he could've done not only for Utrera but as an example to the other towns in the province. It was such that, more than just a memoir of his tenure, it can be considered a public treatise for what can be accomplished by an officeholder with righteousness of principles, energy and firm will.

And from all of the projects he undertook as mayor, he left a detailed record of accounts with his signature on each and every page, so that nobody would take credit for his work nor seek to make false claims of him later on. And ending his years in that capacity, he exhorts his fellow townsfolk to continue improving the city in subsequent administrations, and to not be taken in by promises but to watch for actions.

These are the wishes of a man who expresses his advice to his neighbors in a testament. It appears that his duties to his town didn't cease when he left the office he'd been elected to, in fact his leadership was in demand more than ever. By then after the inheritance from his mother, his sons now owned an important part of the estate; and for them – it was for them, those who had little desire for the quiet life of the Santander mountains, he prepared that grand plantation.

The opportunity comes from the times. These are the years following the famous decree by Mendizabal and the Madoz law. And, as the first one regulated the disbandment of the massive ecclesiastical estates and the second the communes, nobles were allowed to sell up to half of their inherited estates. There was now an abundance of investments and Don Clemente, as others of his day who were possessed of economic possibility, was one of the beneficiaries of this transfer of ownership. This way the new Andalucian *latifundios* were created thus clearly demonstrating the failure of the politics of government.

Don Clemente is convinced, as he himself tells us, that 'ignorance is the cause of society seeing itself invaded by corrupt individuals as they lack the education necessary that would soften their habits, remove them from vices, and incline them towards vocation and work. In this sense I want to leave nothing to be desired; the youth here have a complete education – due originally to the generosity of my relatives Don Francisco de Gibaja and Don Andres Gil de la Torre. For my part, figuring it was the highest good I could do for the town where I was born, once its poverty had been attended to, is the establishment which I solely funded, so that orphaned girls could receive an education free of charge that is worthy of their august mission bequeathed to them by nature."

The school was granted on the 20th of October, 1866, and would be located facing the parochial church, having a rent of 1,666 *reales* per year which Don Clemente himself would pay for from his Encinilla field, and even to this day the school exists and in the entrance one can see a memorial stone to this act.

After a few years, following the custom of the time and carried by the pragmatism of his character, our "grandfather" decides to search for adequate girlfriends for his sons. Don Enrique is destined to be with a young lady having just arrived from Mexico, named Marciala Sainz de la Maza y Gomez de la Puente, who according to reports she had been generously blessed by nature. Federico on the other hand had worse luck. It's known that he complained to his brother and resisted the idea of such an imposition on him at all.

Enrique and Marciala set the date for the 27th of February, 1867 in Rasines, and although the groom had not reached the age of majority (25 years), his father tells him that it is now time to participate (and Federico too) in the responsibilities that are his to administer to. But although these are his words, it doesn't appear to have occurred this way. At the hour of truth, all remains just a theory. Don Clemente doesn't release the reigns so easily. He's already 64 years old, but far from feeling the fatigue of his continual struggle, he appears to continue to have all the strength in the world to keep at it. He buys another farmhouse named 'Berlobrego', along with 317 hectares, the estate 'Haza Grande' near the edges of the village of Moron and the farmlands Torecillas at public auction. All of this he adds to another property 'Alorin', that he had acquired a year before, and being on the borders of his other properties, like the Berlobrego, totals among them all a grand estate surpassing over 600 hectares of 'Caseron' in addition for a total of 5,013 hectares.

Our 'grandfather' being customarily impassioned and fully engrossed in the above task, his son Federico falls ill – he had returned from Belgium having finished his studies as an Agronomist. The sickness is extremely grave, the doctors diagnose him with Meningitis. And Don Federico dies single, at age 24, the 15 of November of '68, without having left a testament to his will.

In the middle of everything, Don Clemente does not cease his business activities and doesn't know when to go about diminishing his acquisitions. Despite his age and his adversities he never considers it opportune to abandon himself to his well deserved rest. Only fifteen days had gone by since the passing of his son and already he is finalizing the terms of a contract to buy several vineyards in the reaches of Montellano and Coronil. Afterwards, he goes about new acquisitions, primarily olive fields, in Utrera, Montellano and Lebrija. His last purchase, the 16th of August of 1871, a house sporting the number 5 on the calle Nueva, in the town of Coronil, bought from Don Diego Villalon Gonzalez, Marquee of Pilares.

At these heights, whether from being conscious of his age or from starting to feel the logical exhaustion of such an unyielding life, Don Clemente wishes to pen his will, spelling out certain partitions which his later circumstances made necessary. He adds from his fist and pen a clause, in effect stating 'his uncles Don Juan Lopez Doriga and Don Simon de Gibaja having died, before writing their wills, like his son Don Federico, our name shall be universally inherited by Don Enrique. And in case the latter passes away before taking possession of the assets, all is to pass to the grandchildren Fernando, Teresa, and any other having been later born, their cousin Don Andres Martinez de la Cuadra should be the executor. He also adds that it is his will that, for his son or he who represents him, to turn over ten *reales* on a daily basis to his sister Feliciana and to her daughter Prudencia, as long as they live, as his appreciation for the care they always demonstrated towards him, and the love with which they helped rear his children. He also notes that should Feliciana and her daughter become separated or impoverished, they are free to live in his house in the Plaza de Gibaja or in the one in Rasines in the Somellera neighborhood, and they should do so without paying rent at all. But if his son Enrique should wish to live in this last house, they should rather occupy the house that is situated across the street in the same place.'

Afterwards, he signs and later rewrites it again nearing the epilogue of his life, he brings clarity in a new clause where he funds a new school for girls in his home town, and arranges for it to be free of tuition to girls and for the teachers to be paid.

In the year 1873, going on nearly 70 years of age, a stubborn companion of his life gave him the irreversible date. The 7th of February, at the onset of night he dies of cerebral apoplexy in his house on Plaza de Gibaja. His eyes closed, the beats of his heart had stopped, and forever gone was his presence. But there remained on the earth his work sprung from years of work and longing. Firm and unforgettable through the ages, just like the statue I saw.

The Life of Clemente de la Cuadra

A true story

Don Clemente de la Cuadra y Gibaja

Original manuscript translated from the Spanish by
Steven Nelson

He had a strong build, neither tall nor short; upright, majestic, with somewhat of a gut and a head on his shoulders. This is how Don Clemente looks in the middle of the plaza, one foot forward, one hand in his pocket, guarding Utrera. His body made of bronze and rusted over, with a green film over the metal which only time can impart, he stands out and can be seen from anywhere in town.

If we look at him from in front, the way you always have to look at people, we'll meet the entrepreneurial Don Clemente, who never gives up a fight, always looking for greater challenges, a leader of men. If we look at him from behind, the way so many insist on looking at him, maybe we'll see the mafioso, the smuggler, the greedy man...it's the price you have to pay in this world if you were a great person, the heads and tails of the same coin, mirroring and forever following those whose names live beyond death.

From in front we'll look at him!

Don Clemente was born the 23rd of November, 1803 in the Rasines province of Santander, Spain. One among eleven children, the commotion must have obviously influenced the course of his destiny. Of all the siblings, we only know about Francisco Javier, Saturnina, Feliciana, Clemente (of whom we're speaking about) and Jose.

The Cuadra family had always lived in Ampuero, small town close to Rasines, likewise important for being the village where the Gibajas sprang from. The families would ally with the marriage of Doña Manuela de Gibaja to Don Juan de la Cuadra Garcia, father of Don Clemente. The close proximity must've made it simple enough for our ancestors to meet one another, and this would be the first time that both surnames would be found together at the same time, and the first time that a Cuadra went to live outside of Ampuero, to that village of Rasines.

Two days after his birth, on the 25th of November, Don Clemente was baptized in the missionary church of Saint Andres. The sacrament was conferred by a brother of his mother, Don Tomas, who at the time was partially supported by that same church. There's a curious note surrounding his godparents, his sister Saturnina and Don Rodrigo Crespo, for having had to take the place of the intended godparents, his maternal aunt and uncle Doña Angela and Don Francisco Javier de Gibaja y Gibaja. She found herself in Utrera and he in Mexico. Coincidentally, it was precisely these two points around which Don Clemente would focus his life. It's as if fate had already chosen then and a mysterious hand had written these two places in the baby's soul.

Around that time there was an infectious desire to go to the New World. Some strange mix of ambition, ingenuity and foolhardiness. It was a desire hard to shake off because it appealed to the deep idealism of man, the almost boyish conviction that they had been born to triumph over the world. America was a great land to follow your dreams, as happens with everything that is seen from afar. Thus it shouldn't seem strange that any father with the slightest connection to America would send his sons there. Practically every son born after the firstborn in Ampuero or Rasines or anywhere nearby was born with his suitcase packed up and a passage in his hand. Seeing as how several of his relatives had already followed this path, Don Francisco, Don Agustin, and Don Manuel de Gibaja Marroquin; brothers of his maternal grandmother, and Don Manuel Viya de Gibaja and Don Francisco de Gibaja y Gibaja had all planted the seeds of adventure for the next generation when they returned rich. This only confirmed the belief that sons were to make their way in the New World, which meant the unappreciated and risky job of being an immigrant.

But Don Clemente carried in his blood the audacity and courage of heroes; men who could not be daunted or dismayed. Men like him could never be placated by the small patch of farm land that his parents owned in the Santander mountains. Small pasture land for livestock like the rest of the folk around Rasines. The longing to be more had probably grown and matured deep in his heart as a reflection of the countless dreams and desires of his ancestors flowing into him. Thus, barely having turned thirteen years old, Don Juan, his father, decided it was time to send him to America. Many years later Don Clemente would give us his tale; we don't know if someone asked him about it in order to go back in time to relive their own youths, or to fill in insatiable hunger to hear a story like his.

"Among all my siblings," says Don Clemente, "by the good grace of divine providence, I have ended up being luckiest among those who have made it to old age; Saturnina, who married Don Damaso Vega, passed away, already having been a widow after a long and painful sickness, leaving five children orphaned and under my protection. Jose, my younger brother, died when he was thirty years old just when life was starting to become favorable, and Feliciana who lives near me with her rather large family, never lacked toil and trouble, until I believe, she could rest assured that she could live the last third of her life in rest and tranquility, and reap the fruits knowing she had favorably found positions and spouses for most of her children.

Since I was little my parents sent me to grammar school, supported by the nobles Don Andres Gil de la Torre y Don Francisco de Gibaja, uncles of mine, and the second one brought to the school Don Manuel Martinez Bustillos, elementary school teacher of a lot of fame, seeing as how he had taught the grand majority of students from Gibaja, Ampuero, Limpias, Velalla, and Ojebar. He also taught Don Santiago and Don Simon, sons of Don Francisco, my uncle.

During the first classes, I went out of my way to show insubordination and be mischievous; and without the healthy force with which I was always corrected, I would have turned out disastrous. However, several episodes which even to this day some neighbors still refer to, and even I remember, show some wit and ingeniousness and that I wasn't without courage and confidence. To illustrate this point I shall give two examples.

In front of our house lived a widowed lady, and in her living room with her children I found myself playing one Sunday while my family had gone to Mass. One of the boys who was with me yelled from the balcony

,Here comes Father Peace!'; who was a layman, an almoner from San Francisco de Laredo, and people said of him that he would take away children whose hands were dirty. Since I happened to be suffering from this defect at the time, and the monk surprised us showing up suddenly, I grabbed the shotgun that was sitting in one of the corners of the living room, I shot at him point-blank. Divine providence saved him, because the gun was heavy and I wasn't strong enough to aim right. The monk escaped taking off running with his robes pulled up, screaming all kinds of obscenities, causing a scandal in town, of which I should have regretted.

Another time, looking for animal nests, I found a rifle that my father had hidden in the hollow of an old chestnut tree, and with it I setup on top of a mound of dirt behind our house. At that time, three or four mule-men strolled by with their droves and carts, and having said to them in a loud voice ,has the mule given birth?', which back then as today is a grave insult to mule-men, who would turn and come at me in a rage, while I, without hesitation, would lift the deadly instrument towards them, point the barrel at them, and would scream at them with a firm voice ,if you come one step closer I'll kill you.' At that moment my dad showed up and what happened afterwards anyone can figure out.

However it happened, by force or on my own, by the time I was eleven I could read, write and count well enough, which was just about all you would learn in school back then. My honorable father then moved me to the house of Don Francisco de Orense y Ravago, an established businessman in Laredo, who occupied me either as a secretary or with household chores, often making me suffer for one reason or another, his violent and impetuous personality. My new boss, however, showed me many times affection with lots of challenges. First he made me study grammar with him, and later on navigation, until around the end of 1816 my esteemed father arranged to send me to New Spain.

The voyage was in and of itself a dangerous proposition. Frequent attacks by land-based pirates endangered even the best defended expeditions. Since I'd embarked on a sixty ton vessel, we passed unnoticed to those prying eyes who must've thought we were a coal-ship from among the islands, and we arrived well. After sixty-some days of sailing, having suffered strong winds and storms, hit by a north wind along the Mexican coastline, what some call ‚the red cheese'.

Upon my arrival in Veracruz, I was met by my honorable uncle Don Manuel de Viya y Gibaja and his family, who showered me with unending attention during the month that I stayed in their home. Afterwards I was on my way to the capital in an armed convoy, as the whole countryside was in revolt, despite the extraordinary measures adopted by Viceroy Don Juan Ruiz de Apodaca, who couldn't quite suppress it.

I spent two years in Mexico (1817-1818). The first was in the famous clothing shop run by Don Francisco Javier de Herreras, hailing from Santander. The second one, at the desk of Don Jose Martinez Barenque, from Rasines, from the Lambera neighborhood, who inaugurated my fortune by blessing me with a salary of one hundred nickels a year.

Señor Barenque was a successful gentleman whose fatherly attention, both his advice and reprimands, made me forgot the inconsiderate treatment I went through in the house of Señor Herreras by the other employees there. Ten years later I would have the pleasure of bailing out some of the more arrogant workers and Herreras himself, after being deported from the Republic of the United States for their multitude of blunders.

Unfortunately the house of Señor Barenque underwent hard times that made him lose clout in the world of business. At the same time, he sent me to the Valley of San Francisco, twelve miles from San Luis Potosi, even though it pained me greatly to leave what I considered my home. Who would've known that later on I would find his only daughter in Cadiz, a beautiful girl, educated in all the subjects, turn up at my doorstep for relief from her poverty.

I spent the whole year of 1820 in the Valley of San Francisco, working in a type of store called a mestiza, where they sell clothes, and serve drinks and meals. But since nothing there offered me what I knew was my destiny, neither the lack of commerce, nor did anyone renowned live there, I was easily swayed by the promises of glory by a native of the land, who resided high in the mountains in Real de Catorce, who brought me there with his group.

Around this time, Odonoju and several other Spanish generals betrayed their fatherland and helped Iturbide in his insurrection and the consummation of Mexican independence. Afterwards, the damage to my fatherland happened right away but the aforementioned generals had their fate decided another day. God would surely want their repugnant ingratitude to suffer later on by another repugnant betrayal.

Arriving at Real de Catorce, it didn't take me long to see that my boss had his head wound up in all kinds of illusions with little grasp of reality. His business revolved around selling clothing to the beneficiaries of the local silver mines. There was a limit to what his skills could do, and my boss had fallen to that fever that takes over all men who become obsessed with silver mines, strangling him with false hopes and backstabbing.

It's not hard to understand that being around this type of sick individual would bring about its fair share of trouble. Surely if you had lived in that kind of a town you would understand, even one in Spain, that being a miner and a visionary were one in the same. I fell prey to the dreams of those more passionate about this than me, and I spent the majority of the year 1821 between 700 and 800 yards underground; exploring and testing, and acting rather imprudently which quite frequently compromised my existence. The only reward that came out of all this was that I had wasted a lot of time and money.

This failure coincided with the death of the wife of my boss, who was a friendly and good woman, and also the future heiress of some great fortune. Seeing my boss plan out his financial future, because his father in law still lived and they had no other heirs, he decided that we should head off to Mazapil, trying to get away from the strict rules of the political class to which he would have to be obedient. Once we'd arrived there, we happened to cross paths with another joker, who managed to bring about once again our excitement for mining, who finally convinced me to stay at the Hacienda de Cedros and dedicate myself to working in one particular mine called "the Cave". But once my boss came back from Parras, where he had gone to rent some equipment, we looked at our ledger and turned out that instead of profits we had losses. And since it turned out that I was a business partner of his, I ended up being in debt for some amount that I'd never even spent. Thus ended our relationship in which I would have never involved myself with if they hadn't tricked me and made me believe that I was going to be owner of villas and castles and owner of a solvent business that never existed.

In the mine "the Cave" I buried my last hopes. And after my business partner disappeared for ever, like magic, I had no other choice but to return to the Valle de Matehuala, where I stayed with his father in law, Don Marcos de la Puente, originally from Ruesga.

Having worked as an assistant in the store of the honorable Don Marcos, an incident occurred that I'll tell you of now, if for no other reason than to record the hard lesson learned from what appeared to be an innocent indiscretion: an old Spaniard named Cosgaya used to come every day to the store who had the habit of asking us for a drink, of course always with the permission of Señor Don Marcos, who liked him a lot. Well, fine, one day we had the bad luck of sprinkling some wood dust, which is a very powerful laxative that the indigenous people here make. The recipient drank the wine without noticing anything, leaving a while later good and healthy like always. But at three in the afternoon, more or less, a doctor ran by us saying that they'd urgently called him from his home. The man had found himself attacked by an extraordinary diarrhea.

Naturally we understood right away the gravity of our actions, after all. We were thinking how we would evade the inevitable consequences to ourselves, when all of a sudden the church bells tolled.

At that point there was no choice but to go as fast as possible to the sick man's house, come out and confess what we did and supply the man with the cold Atole, the known antidote for that kind of venom. I had made myself in charge of recounting our horrid deed, and I learned with glee and surprise, upon arriving at the man's dwelling, the man we'd thought dead, that the church bells did not signal his death but rather that of an even greater afflicted man, and I suffered the abuses and reproach of the family upon making my declarations. The worst part was that the whole episode, being common knowledge and the talk of the town, we were the targets of a lot of sarcasm for quite a few days. Amen that my patron dished out the deserved punishment, not withstanding that the old man later fully recovered.

The respectable Señor Gomez de la Puente thought so highly of me after not having been at his service for long, so much so that he made me the administrator in charge of his estate at Pastoriza. I was barely even eighteen years old and I ventured without the knowledge and prudence that comes with experience. He made sure I omitted nothing; to make sure my work was reliable while I managed his interests during those two years. And apart from a few small improprieties, he had no reason to regret it. But his wife, proud and foolish, who also dominated him, used to like start rumors and always felt it necessary to harass the workers. Seeing as how it wasn't in my character to put up with such vilification I felt the need to leave the position to my assistant who had already found himself tied up in the aforementioned drama as well as for other more indignant reasons.

From Matehuala, I left for Tampico de Tamaulipas, that was being built around that time (1823), and I owed no small amount of gratitude to Don Jose and Don Fermin de la Lastra who lived in Altamira and Pueblo Viejo, located near each other.

In Tampico I stayed long enough to convince myself that there was no position there that I wanted, and I left for Tuspam, that same year 1823, looking for the protection of Don Juan del Juncal, who occupied an advantageous position there. And sure enough, he received me in his house with the same affection he would show to someone just born.

Almost immediately Juncal sent me to Veracruz as shipmate of one of his cargo vessels (the San Cayetano), in order to receive a shipment, in said place, of fruit that it carried and to return afterwards with the goods having been converted into money. The mission accomplished, I returned to everyone's satisfaction, but bad fortune wished upon me that during the business exchange in the narrow sea inlet of Tuspan, they hurled a bale of goods from the gunwale when they were loading, and it flipped over the canoe that I was in and I fell into the cold water. Afterwards I caught a fever that lasted until the end of 1824.

During this unfortunate time period, the most pathetic of my life, the suffering and privations reached the extreme. It's true that Señor Juncal never failed to give me the deserved care; whenever I felt able I would make myself useful by managing the ledgers of his business, and later when there was a new store opening, he sent me to manage it and I carried out the task flawlessly. But one day, feeling desperate about my health, I took off to Campeche to look for relief by changing the temperature around me, not only did he not compensate me for my management of his store, but he also charged me for the costs incurred while I was sick and even the little that I had borrowed to make the trip.

Once again I embarked anew, and the ordeal was so difficult that more than once the results thereof brought me to the gates of death and the merchant thought it prudent to drop me off upon arrival and intern me in the hospital of San Juan de Dios to spend there the last hours that remained of my existence.

Upon my internment at that establishment, instantly Don Pedro Manuel Rodriguez came to visit me, originally from a town called Arnuero, of whom he was the merchant who did business there. Since he was an honorable man and a generous man, and my youth and visage enchanted him, he made the top doctor himself come take care of me, who was called Gallegos, who confirmed that my diagnosis was fatal and that any medical care would be useless.

This not withstanding, he administered to me some spiritive drink that revived my senses, and with them the faculty to explain the causes of my ailment, which were not the ones that they had presumed, and instead were ones that had commenced with intermittent fever and continued to reoccur tenaciously over the months, had taken away my appetite and created an invincible repugnance to any and all foods, of any kind. From there my weakness drove me to the deplorable situation in which I found myself.

A black slave took charge of rehabilitating my completely extinguished strength with a soup especially prepared by the doctor. The african discharged his mission fantastically and continually offered me the prodigious sustenance that I got out of religious faith, as apparently during my trance I never lost hope. After twenty four hours I was already another man.

At that time Señor Rodriguez transferred me to the house of some ladies who took charge of taking care of me. They did it very effectively and my convalescence was visible to the naked eye. But bad luck at the time, which during those days, the Yucatans, who were at war with the Campechanos, came close to our city and bombed it incessantly. Divine Providence at that time exposed me to a new and clear danger.

After the campaign ended, I found myself much more fit and with a pair of crutches I was skipping around the grounds. And before two months passed I decided to return straight to Tuspan.

I attributed my ungodly recovery to a frightful resolution I had taken. During the depression I felt myself in as a consequence of the intensity and obstinacy of the suffering my arms and legs became crippled. To the point that I'd had to be fed by a stranger's hand. In this lamentable state, the head doctor paid me a normal visit, and after the questions about my strength and having spent some time with me, he went right away to the next room over, where the nurses were, they interrogated him over my health, wishing to know whether they could maintain hope of my recovery, he said simply : "For God, nothing is impossible."

I heard this mistake, and I called for him. When he was before me I told him: "To get healthy, if God wishes, I don't need you. I hope that you won't visit me anymore. I want you to know that I won't take anything that you prescribe me because I'm convinced that you know nothing of what ails me, and before continuing to suffer by trusting in your ignorance, I'd rather trust in Divine Providence even if I succumb."

Then, the man muttered some words, and to my harsh words he responded by taking off, irritated like a madman. I kept on by refusing all the concoctions that the doctor had tried to heal me with, for naught. Neither the pleadings of the owners, nor the advice and reprimands of the concocter, nor the prudent observations of other people, were enough to make me give up my resolve. From that moment on, renouncing every medicine, I did nothing more than sustain myself with whatever foods appealed to me the most. Then, I started the exercise and training as soon as I felt better, making fun of the false prophets, determined to start my journey to the continent.

Determined, I tell you, I loaded my baggage in the schooner San Cayetano that belonged to Juncal. But, a couple hours before we set off, the same Captain that had taken me to Campeche showed up. And delighted to find me alive, he insisted unconditionally that I make the trip on his ship. I resisted as much as I could since I had everything already on board, but, without asking permission, he had his servant pick up my bags and he insisted so strongly that I had no choice but to accept. I thus freed myself from a certain death. Without knowing, I had abandoned a ship whose destiny was to wreck during this trip.

In Tuspam, it didn't take me long to recuperate fully, and not taking me long to figure out that nothing or next to nothing could prosper in the house of Señor Juncal, as he made sure to monopolize any and all business. I decided then to take a position that a merchant from Pueblo Viejo offered me, and even though the business was quite pitiful, surely due to the unique personality of my new boss, in turn it brought me a decent income that let me save a little. And when I had a thousand nickels, I opted for independence.

With absolute ownership of myself, my first task was, naturally, to choose the means to make myself rich quick. And since the occasion happened to come by me at that moment in Tampico, to buy red wine, that in San Luis de Potosi had an exorbitant price, I decided to purchase fifty barrels, which cost me the previously mentioned sum of money, more or less. And I dispatched them to Don Juan Zabalardo, who was one of the richest dealers at that time with a great network, along with some competent people.

Even though the wine arrived at its destination late and thus deteriorated, I was told that they had sold seven barrels for forty four nickels, which paid for the shipment, the wages and other expenses, and that forty three other barrels waited in storage for another bidder.

Meanwhile, as I awaited the results, giving repeated orders to sell the inventory which were not heeded, when I started to become impatient for want of something to do, at the beginning of 1825, a proposition from Señor Juncal came to distract me. He wanted me to take charge of a shipment of pepper and sarsaparilla that he wanted to ship abroad. As soon as I heard, I took off to Tuspam, I worked day and night to gather the cargo that was valued at over twelve thousand nickels, and I followed the orders of Don Jose de Lastra who had legal power from Juncal to act as he saw fit with it. My effort would be compensated with three thousand nickels upon our return. That's to say, with one fourth of the profit that this investment produced. A paltry sum with which my friend thought he was justly compensating me, and which in another situation I would have refused indignantly.

Arriving in New York without incident on the ship Altamaria after having spent the March equinox in the ocean, an omen which portented various failings, I sold the cargo at a profit and purchased from the markets there those products I figured to be most advantageous, I returned with the same merchant ship to Tampico. Furthermore, completely separate from the merchant cargo I had ordered, I carried 2822 pesos that a merchant had lent me on credit and which Don Francisco de la Maza had guaranteed, that old and good friend.

The expedition had been a total success. Upon our arrival we found the plaza deserted and we were able to conduct our business without problems of any sort. Consequently, the profits were quite handsome, and to my benefit almost three thousand nickels corresponded to me. However, since during my absence Don Juan Zabalardo had embarked to Europe and his brother-in-law whom he had left in charge of his business was just a figurehead who never attended to the assets nor liabilities, finally it went bankrupt and all the creditors stood mocked and left with nothing, myself among them. And thus I saw disappear, all at once, the bruised dreams of a poor man, the first and most difficult twenty thousand *reales* of my fortune.

This last expedition being complete, Mr. Juncal sent word for me to join him in a new venture that he intended to make to France. Later on, after finding out all I could about fruits, which was the commodity we were dealing with, I did not wish to join this endeavor. He only wished to split one third of the profits with me, and seeing as how it required me to put up all of my money, I would be working for free, more or less. Nevertheless, I continued to work in his home and acted as his representative in his absence.

Meanwhile, some friends of mine organized an expedition from Tuspan, with the pretense of going to the ports of North America, which originally would've been headed to Havana, which the Republic was at war with. The job was very risky, but offered some advantages in turn. Since Spanish products were prohibited in Mexican territory and likewise being infinitely desired by the locals, they traded for fabulous prices when one managed to introduce them disguised as foreign products.

These speculators thought of me to be their front man. And notwithstanding the wise observations of those who understood the dangers I exposed myself to, including Mr. Juncal who gave me numerous and strong reasons to dissuade me, including invoking my dreams with the hope that he would make me his business partner one day, I ventured forward without any hesitation, dragged by some secret force that has always led me towards difficult fights.

I gained a favorable salary, and after requesting a loan in order to augment my cargo, I had a salary of 3200 that was coming to me for completing one job.

Under these wonderful conditions I marched my way to the island of Cuba on the brigantinee Hero. And although I intended to trade separately, I pooled my capital with that of Perez and the others because that way we all benefited more from our purchases; this in spite of the shenanigans they pulled on me at the last minute – it was miserable. But my desire to work and prove myself was enormous.

In Havana, Perez' lack of experience and general idiocy put me in the position of having to do all the trading myself. But it let me select one of the most exquisite cargos for the mexican markets, and, in the same ship, we headed to customs to present our false papers and present ourselves as Americans.

But in order to do this it was necessary to unload the ship and pay the tariff. At that point we realized that the floor of the ship was completely rotten making it impossible to continue the voyage. But one of the shipbuilders was with me, Galician by birth, called Pepon Perez, who even though he couldn't read was a clever man and very street smart. He told me that with a few repairs we could continue. And to persuade me that we would go on safely, he signed a contract guaranteeing any damages that might happen to the goods on the way back to Mexico. My innocence reigned supreme, it did not let me realize how little we would've cared of such guarantees if we ended up capsizing.

At that moment and from the same port, a schooner called Antoinette de Pereira took off destined for Tampico, and I made sure that our papers had the same destination because there was a Colombian Corsair anchored next to us who observed our movements with poorly disguised intentions. Later on I'll explain why.

The Antoinette and the Hero made off to sea together. The Corsair remained in stream, we followed the schooner and made it to Tuspam even though we had no sea-men except for the Captain who was total drunk since the pilot had gotten off right before takeoff.

Anchored in port, and it being impossible to enter due to the draught, let's remember that the Captain and Pepon had disembarked in order to fill out some superfluous paperwork for Juncal, which Pepon had hidden in his shoes. I stayed on board in order to direct the unloading on the condition that they verify the paperwork at once and that they send me some fresh food which we lacked since the Galician preferred penny pinching.

Eight days passed without hearing anything from land, and anyone who knows how easy it was to ruin somebody back then for the sole crime of being born a Spaniard; if you had heard of the repugnant activities of the so-called Jauregui, who at the time was a military commander of that district; you would easily understand my anxious situation which foreboded my absolute destruction.

On daybreak of the ninth day, they augmented my fright by several cannon shots coming from the ocean, landing not a short distance from where we floated. Not long after we saw a schooner come closer that had just shouted. It was the warship Papaloapam, fleeing from Tampico to Veracruz carrying one hundred gunners and twenty six women, and having lost their rudder, they found themselves forced to call for help.

They threw out the anchor and the commander came to speak with me so that we would pick up the passengers. But I managed to only allow the women to board us, as I protested that the soldiers might commit some transgressions on my ship, and seeing as how we were in such proximity to them, it would be easy to come to their aid, if need be. Agreeing to this, and while the females were being transported over, with their luggage, dogs, cats, parrots and all the belongings that accompany Mexican soldiers, on this small boat going back and forth to the Papaloapam, while they discussed how to bring the schooner in port to repair the equipment. And in the last trip, at dusk, a man named Roque Garcia, a Mallorcan, came to speak with me. Even though he was half inebriated, he told me frankly, passing by me, that Juncal had sent him to warn me that all was lost and that I should do whatever I wanted.

Surprised by his demeanor and by the way this news arrived to me, I tried to make him explain things to me, but I couldn't get anything out of him other than „there's no hope at all; the Captain and Pepon are locked in a cell, and if they catch you they will shoot you for sure."

This news confirmed my fears, now it was inevitable that my suspicions would come true, I found myself in the desperate situation of a man in a chapel having just been condemned to death. Because, escape was impossible - the villain on land who wanted my demise would surely order the commander of the warship Papaloapam to fire on me, it didn't even appear rational. And expecting justice or mercy from he who wanted to take my cargo so bad he would murder me in order to satisfy his disgusting vices, vices which dominated him, would've been crazy. God, who sometimes allows bad people to get away with things to test the faith and resolve of the good, did not intend for the criminal intentions of Jauregui to be realized.

The insomnia caused by my situation gave me such fatigue that I spent the entire night delirious until the dawn, spilling her light over the horizon, came to change the scene. The pilot came and told us that the Papaloapam had to hold anchor until the tides calmed before entering port. They took the women on shore, relieving of me the greatest burden I had ever felt in my life, and as soon as I began to breathe in a semblance of relief, when the glimmer of a new day's brilliant light began to illuminate my lost cause once again, the naval commander came on board and informed me that they wanted to arrest me on land, and being an employee of that nation, he was in charge of arresting me and placing me before the courts.

By chance, having foreseen such a situation, I received the news with indifference, outwardly at least. Despite the fact that they were going to lock me up, take away my liberty and my greatest dreams, probably forever. I concentrated my faculties and making a supreme effort, guided by necessity, I managed to convince him that he had no need to worry, because I fully intended to present myself to the local authorities the following day. In order to avoid any doubts and to exaggerate the needless efforts he would have to go through, since I found myself under a foreign flag, I managed to dissuade him to wait until tomorrow.

At that moment, hesitating would not suffice. The situation was quite tenuous, and I either had to surrender myself or play this cat and mouse game to perfection. At twenty three years of age and feeling very passionate, the choice that I would take was long ago decided. But without the ship's crew, all would be lost. And since they were all Americans, and the only one I understood was the cook, the black African who spoke English and Spanish, through his intermediation the crew understood that the Captain and the Galician had been imprisoned, and the same fait awaited us all if they caught us. And having painted for them an accurate depiction of the anguish of captivity, I proposed to them that we head off to Tampico to save ourselves, something which they, of course, accepted.

Under these circumstances, when the time came for morning prayer, I invited the commander and all of the naval officers of the Papaloapam to tea on our ship. I offered them the best that I had and on top of that there were games and gin, to which they were greatly inclined. At around ten, assisted by Virgo and Bacchus, I managed to get them all back to their boat, mostly drunk, and I along with them, not before having taken a few bottles with me to finish the job. We drank the most boiling liquor, flushed with hurrahs, and sang the most belligerent patriotic songs, as one after the other began losing consciousness.

Around noon more or less, I returned to my ship, after first having made sure that all the guards on the Papaloapam were sound asleep, taking advantage of the unconsciousness of their bosses. And without wasting a minute, I put the whole crew to work on our task. In silence, we lifted anchor, passed by the warship, covered in fog, we avoided wrecking ourselves on the jagged rocks, they had never looked so big. After two days we had made it to the port of Tampico in record time.

Determined to avoid being boarded, we hoisted the French flag, and made like we were busy until a tugboat approached, and a guy called Pepe Quero came out, having been expressly sent by Commander Jauregui to find out the name of our Captain, where we came from, etc., etc. and to arrest us if we were the crew of the Hero, which they were expecting. But since they didn't recognize our ship, and I had repainted the hull a different color, I told them in poor Spanish, pretending to be a foreigner, that our ship was the Elizabeth of Burgeos, that our captain was sick in the cabin and named Garnier and that we came from Veracruz (our ship only had half a load), to pick up a shipment of lumber here if it was ready. That I was the pilot and we would enter the port on the next day, if the principal of the ship so ordered me.

As they waited for me to pay my merchant's fee, and as I surreptitiously negotiated my intention to do business, some of the men from the tugboat were telling me about this guy Cuadra who had escaped from the wharf at Tuspam with the schooner Hero, having left its Captain imprisoned, and that they had been ordered to place him under arrest if he arrived in Tampico and to confiscate his cargo since it came from a foreign land. And ready to do so were two platoons waiting on shore, since a certain Colombian Corsaire had warned that the Hero would be arriving to port at any moment if the Corsaire didn't catch it out at sea, which it was looking to do.

Taking this into account, my first thought was to get rid of the cargo with all haste; to avoid that they discover it by chance. I had the cook, who had heard everything, go speak with the crew and agree on a course of action. They had to know that the Colombian pirates could reappear at any time and it was necessary to make a decision to avoid a confrontation.

I've already mentioned the condition of our ship. We lacked food and water, none among us was a seaman, and even though I had studied some in my early years I didn't remember anything. Lastly, none among us had ever been in New Orleans, which was the natural destination that a Frenchman would be headed to. Nevertheless, it was essential that we decide since there was no middle ground; either we resign to be victims of the perverted Jauregui, for whom our misfortune would be his glory, or we could wait to be captured by the pirates who would dispossess us of our goods and dispose of us. Or, we could throw ourselves back out to sea without reservation, with our eyes blinded to our course and at the mercy of the heavens and the waves, to search through the terrible elements of this desert the protection and asylum that the land refused us.

Although such disconcerting options only served to augment the uncertainty of our lives, we all instinctively decided for the last choice without a doubt. It was the only one that offered some hope. We made ourselves believe that time would benefit us, and at some point a ship traveling back from the United States would take us to a port. Nonetheless the results convinced us that we hadn't counted on being long-term guests.

We straightened the bow towards where we wished, with a brisk wind, taking the precaution of fasting without which we would have perished, as we will see, and once we had made it out a-ways, we lost track of time and some of us our sanity, during which we spent twenty days rowing hard but making no headway. A furious southern wind came and put us in a dire situation. I assure you the anguish engulfed us and there were those of us who saw their final moments written above in the sky. The sails and rigging couldn't resist the storm. They were smashed, and we found ourselves forced out to sea, for four or five days, to avoid condemning ourselves.

Once the storm subsided, I thought we were near the island of Cuba, which was very dangerous to the restrictions. We kept turning around until we thought we had the right course, having a tough time of it due to the dense sea and constant squalls, so much so that it took fifteen days before we saw land. There was a point where we didn't know where we were, which offered us both the opportunity and likewise the risk that there was no more than four yards to the bottom and not too far from the beach. We worried about running aground, and from coming and going, here and there, we spent another twenty days halted.

Having no choice, our dismay started to spread despite trying to stay positive. We'd gone over a month at two crackers and one quart of water per person and we had nothing left but the crumbs that we managed to gather, enough water for another day and no wood left to navigate.

This was the condition we were in when we thought we saw a port. It was without a doubt either Galveston or Barataria. But even though we fired our cannon thirty times, after 48 hours of being visible, nobody came out and we could see nothing. At that point some on board proposed a reconnaissance with the small boat, to see if they found a fort of some kind, but I opposed this as I feared that they would desert and leave the rest of us abandoned. Others wanted us to come ashore and march inland, but again I dissuaded them because of the risk of being caught by indians. And at last, helped by a little bit of "fire water" that I managed to supply through our cook-translator, who did his job well, they agreed that come life or death we would row back out to sea, all night and the following day to see if we would find another vessel to come to our aid.

It just so happened that with an 8 miles per hour wind, and after thirty hours more or less, following constantly the same pace, as the afternoon began to dusk, we discovered on the horizon another schooner under the lee from whom we requested help by flag and cannon blast. She steered closer to the wind, we came alongside with our sails down, and in the blink of an eye we were within trumpet distance. They shouted that they were the Satiana coming from Matamoros, and having told them of our situation, they helped us very generously to whatever we needed, except a pilot as they only had one, according to tradition in that profession. However, they did offer to sail in convoy, which we did, entering the Mississippi two days later through the S.O. pass.

At once upon throwing anchor the head of custom came out to us. And seeing as how we had no cargo and no papers, as it had all remained in Tuspam, he sent us under guard to the customs house. Upon our arrival in New Orleans, which was at a distance of thirty leagues from the entry of the river, our arrival was already known due to telegraph, and among the mass of Spaniards that awaited me there at the pier, I was pleased to hug first my always good friend Don Fernando de la Lastra, who like everyone else, had supposed I was dead. Not long later, Mr. Glover presented himself, captain of the Hero, having been set free, due to the intervention of the American diplomat, he had come to find me and recommended that I consign the goods of Don Simon Cuasllu, a merchant here.

And thus ended a campaign brought about through imprudence and a lack of reflection, continued by fear, and brought to a happy conclusion by Divine Providence. But so that the story be complete and neither the narration nor the events appear unbelievable, nor the circumstances of having navigated American waters for sixty days without our mast breaking, nor the privations of so much time on crackers and water, we should therefore add some things. First, during the voyage the crewmen had had their own goods intended for sale, which represented their life savings, and because of that, them as well as I, we accepted whatever resolution to our troubles no matter how disheartening; second, that without knowing it, we had spent a lot of time in the waters that form the bay of Saint Bernard with the Colorado river, and due to this region being inhabited by savages, and not being a frequented route, it could have very well ended up with our lying there with the world not knowing, and thirdly, due to the privations we went through, having weighed myself before embarking on this voyage and once again upon my arrival in New Orleans, the difference was twenty three pounds less.

Despite finding myself rather lifeless, the first couple days I busied myself with disembarking the few goods we had, as per the orders of the original partners. I spoke with various vendors directly regarding my situation and business, I chartered a new ship because the Hero was condemned and sold as unfit to sail. I arranged what I needed and immediately after (around July) I sent the new goods to Tampico consigned to Don Jose de la Lastra.

Finally having completed this business, I didn't have much of a choice but to stay in New Orleans, as there was no way I could appear in Tampico at the head of the return expedition. Also, during my absence, the conspiracy of Padre Arenas was discovered in Mexico, in which the wicked Jauregui accused me of being complicit, and many had died at the gallows, the same friar, General Arana, and a whole lot of others. But I can swear that I had nothing to do with that, and that during my stay in the country I had no other occupation but earning a fortune to return to my dear homeland. In reality, what Jauregui was looking for was to confiscate my ship and its cargo and the satisfaction of putting me, the man who had fooled him previously, before a firing squad.

Upon ending the business, so that each partner received what his share, I believed that all would recognize without a fuss the obligation to compensate me for my services that I had rendered. I made sure to stress it to Sr. Lastra, as well as others, who had other intentions, assured me of my compensation until the moment that they had theirs, and afterwards, they reneged on their word, taking advantage of my absence in Mexico. There was more still; so that their perfidy would be complete, Don Juan de Juncal, with whom I had pooled together funds, took 2718 duros which belonged to me (less 282 which was my share of the losses), and even though I must have written him a hundred times, that I was sick as a result of the labor and privations of the voyage; even though I belabored the dictionary for words to beg and make him recognize a duty that honor and conscience should dictate - yet when he responded, it was to tell me to find an occupation so I could survive on my own.

I don't know if Juncal conceived of the miserable idea of keeping what was mine at that moment. What I can tell you is that he employed the most shameful means of doing so; regardless of my diligence in taking care of our business and resorting to all kinds of unimaginable things to make a profit. I did not get what was mine until August of 1837, ten years later, when he was ordered to indemnify me my sum by an arbiter we had agreed on.

Fortunately, when I arrived in New Orleans, the eminent, generous and good countryman Don Simon Cuenllu, originally from Mandaca, took me into his house. And I say fortunately, because without his hospitality, and lack of health, with no economic means at all and in a country whose language I did not know, I would have seen myself irremissibly leading a precarious existence. I collaborated with him with what I could, and during my free time I studied French, I soon found myself able to make it on my own.

My first resolution was to write to Don Jose de la Lastra asking to borrow 1,000 duros, which he sent me right away. With them and the support of Sr. Cuenllu, I took my first step, building a grocery store of quite high quality; and I began to work again, from dawn until midnight to repair what my adversity and weakness had damaged.

Thus established, it's just to say that the results reversed not only my previous misfortunes, but after a year I had acquired excellent credit with my vendors. Even to the point of taking whatever I wished from their warehouses to fill my shop, discounting my rate at the banks, like as a capitalist.

I found myself among such auspices when the expulsion of Spaniards from Mexico occurred. It was surely an act of ingratitude without equal among history, as no son had ever thus demeaned the sacrifices of his parents, though for me, it became a factor in my prosperity as it multiplied my profits immensly. Young, old, women and children, rich and poor, men of means and the most humble, all piled together and driven off, in not much better conditions than the blacks from Africa, to New Orleans. Mercilessly thrown out of their own dwellings by their own kin; by those who owed them their own existence, their religion, their culture, customs, the name that they carried, and even the color that made them often vain. And everyone instinctively came to me, to find them accommodation, to act as an interpreter, to help with difficulties both personal and peculiar, with the only benefit to me being their consumption in my store. But as it was highly regarded, and the number of outcasts at that time large, and the vast majority came with metal, and as among them were many ordinary men and I was there to exploit the situation I built a boarding house, an inn, with billiards, a tavern, and all kinds of games; including Faraon, B(G)uleta, and Monte; and as all these took place during both day and night, and as idleness is the mother of all deviations among men, in very little time I had amassed over 10,000 duros.

Meanwhile, in the port of Havana, a war expedition was being readied against the Republic of Mexico, commanded by General Barradas, who became famous, despite the blunders of his offensive. It was said at the time that when he insisted on attacking, the authorities in Cuba resisted many times, and at last the influence of ignorance had triumphed as well as the perversity that dominated their courts. Be that as it may, the reality is that three thousand men gathered on those ships, some local and some foreign, and they made off to sea in a convoy headed by a man-of-war and other battle ships, at the command of the arrogant admiral Laborda. It was known that the squadron left without many of the precautions typical of such a venture; such as they didn't even have Spanish retreat specialists (piloto de derrota) on their ships, to avoid total confusion, nor was there a rally point designated in case of a rout, and due to this unpardonable carelessness, the American frigate Golconda was able to detach itself from the fleet with five hundred men, having made the captain, a pure soldier and always seasick, believe that they had just saved themselves from certain danger, surely as they left the port they were bought and paid by the republicans to do what they did. And on top of that disaster, instead of taking their soldiers to the spar of Tampico or near it, something which would have been convenient for those familiar with the area, the landing occurred at Punto de Jerez and Cabo Rojo, twelve leagues away from the Tampico, ushering in the utter disgraceful catastrophe of which we will deal with later.

Let's leave the crown's soldiers jumping on shore, at Punta Jerez, for a moment and let's follow the sail of that lost ship which arrived in New Orleans feigning it had experienced thunderstorms and troubles without end. The troops quartered themselves in a building commandeered by the Governor of the region, and the consul was sent to notify the Spanish authorities in Cuba seeing that, having passed a certain amount of time, the very same General Laborda showed up at the port, with the Asia, the Restauracion, and the Cautivo, to take them to their destination.

The circumstances should've advised Laborda to reembark his troops and lead them without delay to the position of Berradas on the Mexican coasts. But the General, deceived by the incense, festivities and feasts that the indigenous of New Orleans showed upon him, he forgot his obligations, and he didn't depart until forty days had passed.

Among the refugees, the invasion engendered enthusiasm. There were many who took up arms to join the expedition. But I, not a part of them, saw myself being drawn by the benefits that a daring speculator might find in the new conquests and, more than anything, by the recommendations of certain persons who awarded me the task of provisioning of the army. I sold my store, and taking a good profit from the condition I left it in, I put forth the funds to purchase foods, and I headed on a ship to Tampico with some other civilians, whom were being driven by bad luck as was I, along the path of pleasant delusions.

While we sail our boats to their destination, without notable trouble, let's return to Cabo Rojo to reconnect with the events that play a part in our story: the poor soldiers of Corona, with their chief out front, jumped out onto the hot sand of the beaches, in the dead heat of summer, underneath one of those suns that seem to envelope nature, on one of those scalding hot days that baked the rocks, in which the white hot fierce air one breathes like bonfires, the poor soldiers of the regiment of Corona, I repeat, marched along the coast, burdened by the weight of their weapons, their equipment and munitions. In that desert, there were no mules available, nor any more water to drink than the brackish water you find when digging a hole near the ocean. And after going through a skirmish at the place called Los Conchos, they arrived at the spar, and found the abandoned fort and all the canons destroyed.

From the beachhead they marched on Tampico, and overcoming the small obstacles that the defenders had put in their way, they took over the plaza, they drove off Garza de Altamira, despite the fact that he commanded three times the troops, and finally, upon returning from one of the many inland expeditions during which they were always victorious, they came out victorious, capturing Santa Anna with his entire division, during his attack on the small guard in the city.

With control of Santa Anna, who was by then the most famous general of the Republic, Barrada, would've undoubtedly made his own name famous by sending the Mexican general to Havana. But the imbecile let himself be deceived during a conference the two of them had. Santa Anna made him believe that the independence of Mexico was impossible to satisfy the people, and that he was resolved to support the intentions of Spain, that Mexico ought to submit itself to her domination once again. That in this sentiment he had the support of the republican army, and that he hoped to be let free to realize his plan, which would occur at once. The Spanish general, more honorable than intelligent, believed in this fraud. He ignored whom he was dealing with, someone not known from justice or decorum, who was well known for his immorality and fallaciousness. And not only did he allow him to return with his troops to Pueblo Viejo, on the other side of the river, but there are actually people who swear that he supported him monetarily, which the traitor said he required.

The moment Santa Anna found himself free, he ordered Barrandas to surrender, via a taunting communique that would've embarassed even a field sergeant. At that point ensued extraordinary times, which flooded the barracks and the warehouses, with a loss of the majority of my goods, completely halting my operations. And while an attack would've defeated our enemy, who was completely disorganized, the consequences of the absurd landing at Punta de Jerez and Cabo Rojo made impossible any assault as that horrible heat, the brackish water, the unbelievable exhaustion, the humidity and the privations, drove to the hospitals four fifths of the Spanish forces, leaving behind to defend the city less than five hundred men.

The presence of such a disconsoling scene bewildered the General, who feared being left without a single healthy man, since the scurvy and fevers were wreaking havoc, and that's the only way that can explain the capitulation, in which their arms were lowered and flags turned over, without having lost a single battle. But the most unheard of part of it was not the surrender of our army nor the joy with which the mexicans hung up the Spanish standard in their congress notwithstanding having been battered and humiliated during each encounter on the field, rather that the capitulation was not understood, not by those who accompanied the division as volunteers, nor the speculators, nor that battalion that had gone missing in the Golanda, since nobody even remembered them.

Santa Anna, with his court, took control of Tampico. And the unpunished murder of several innocents was the first sign of the kind of protection and security that was in store for those who'd surrendered. The infamy did not stop at that: during a banquet that same day, the federals were celebrating their glorious triumph, they agreed to a surprise attack on the detachment at the small fort of la Barra, which had not heard of the surrender having been without communication for some time now. And drunk with pleasure at the thought of finally being victorious over the castilian army, even though their success was due to vile treachery, a thousand men volunteered, and those officers who had distinguished themselves so well in the salons and the bars due to their shyness of confronting the sons of Spain now placed themselves at the forefront of this expedition, flushed due to the whiskey being doled about at that time.

The fortress was impetuously attacked in the dark, and although the guard held one hundred and fifty valients, much of them sick with fever, including Colonel Vazquez who commanded, they resisted fearlessly several different assaults, and the fields already covered and the ditches filled with more than five hundred cadavers, among them almost all of the authors of this criminal enterprise, the pressured defenders of the fort were not content with heroically stopped the aggression, but they then went on the offensive, they abandoned their trenches upon hearing the voice of their commander Vizarro, who didn't leave his post even when pegged by a bullet, and charging by bayonet over the enemy survivors, they chased them a great distance, abandoning them at last to their appropriate ignominy where history would castigate them.

Having been skewered, just as they had planned on skewering ours, they told our men of the capitulation, and after an official had gone to make certain of this, they accepted the surrender on the condition that they not turn over their arms until they moment they vacated the territory. The battalion from New Orleans arrived at the scene of the catastrophe after these events had occurred. Barradas sought refuge in the United States, only to die later on in Paris of his own misery. And I never received word that the government in Madrid ever sought to punish in any way, those whose failed methods precipitated the calamity of the venture which should've had good results for Spain. Not because I think the conquest of the Republic an easy task, rather that the victory of Tailor at the head of an undisciplined mob has come to demonstrate evidently what our soldiers should've been capable of, being commanded by Arredondo or by another experienced soldier, who knew the terrain and the customs of the natives.

Immediately after having consummated this tragedy over the Tamaulipas war, which we have covered since my own personal fortunes were involved, the boat in which I was on and the ones who headed the retreat stopped in Tampico, and we all knew with surprise and heartache the lamentable state of our compatriots. We stayed a few days at the spar watching over the embarkment of the troops, and having finished this operation, we set off to Havana, where we arrived dismantled due to a fierce storm which caused substantial damage among the warships.

Since it was natural after two months of hardship, after disembarking my goods, a good portion of them were in bad shape. And thus it was just able to satisfy an indemnification that could not be covered, even though what was left we sold fairly well, in a public auction, it was barely enough to cover the costs and the freightage.

Fortunately, the man who had purchased my establishment in New Orleans still owed me two thousand duros, without which this would be the third time that I would find myself penniless. I marched there, and it turns out that during this tragic period, my purchaser had passed away and his widow had no interest in business, I decided to take it over once again. We came to an agreement, and I kept the business on very reasonable conditions, and above all else without having to pay a premium.

After my reestablishment, I renewed my connections with the business community, managing to recuperate everything I had lost through hard work and the economy, despite the circumstances not being the same now that Spaniards were allowed reentry in the Republic and the amount of consumers fell. I sold my business again and headed to Tampico where my brother Jose was living, young and full of the hope of what his great abilities had in store, especially notable was his seriousness and moderation, and very notable as he spoke and wrote English and

French with the same perfection as Castilian, thanks to having attended an American college for two years, paid for by me.

The welcome I received in Tampico when I arrived was the best. Those who had returned earlier and who knew me had taken it upon themselves to speak of me very highly and placed a halo on my reputation which, according to them, was merited due to my services in New Orleans. Then, just as I had decided, I started the best grocery store that existed there during that era, I brought my brother with me, and I worked without wasting any time at all, my prosperity continually growing, until an unexpected event cut short the rapid return of my fortune.

Near the end of 1832 or early 1833, the so called liberals staged a coup in the area of Tamaulipas. And this name has been usurped by so many, here and in other places, by those who wanted to take control of public institutions to live at the expense of others; they took advantage of the innocence of the townsfolk to present themselves as supreme patriots; and came to power under the pretense of abolishing taxes and tariffs which never came about, and dragged the rest of us into ruin and loss.

The incendiary revolution quickly spread to our place, as it was always the first task of any rebellion to take over a port with which to import foreign goods without tariffs to finance their activities. And a stubborn man named Tomas Rosell, son of Campeche although a cataluñan native, who never ceased to gloss over his own iniquities in the name of patriotism, having later made himself the leader of the insurgents, he soberly decreed that all Spaniards were to be expelled, giving them eight days to arrange their belongings.

Such arbitrary action made the victim's situation all the more dangerous, as there were now fewer people one could trust. In such unfortunate situations there was a man who gave his desk to his indigenous dependant, who ended up betraying him, who ended up turning over his store to his wife, who was later tricked as she did not understand anything; who passed on her assets to a local under certain conditions which were never fulfilled, and who took residence with a native godson of hers, who owed her everything, and upon the husband's return found his house burnt to the ground. Don Jose de la Lastra had left his wealth and turned over his businesses to an Italian named Avesana who threw everything out the window, bringing his benefactor in disgrace and later ruin. I sold what I had to a Veracruzano, who offered me no guarantees of its return except his word, on the condition that I pay him five hundred duros monthly, and my brother, who at the insistence of a lady of influence was spared from exile, would not have been able to take over my operations. And it pained me again as I was certain that this would be the fourth time that I would be wounded again with misfortune.

Forced thus by threats to abandon our businesses and relationships, and not having anything but the brigantine Aguascalientes, dischartered through age, we had no choice but to embark on this condemned ship, because neither reason nor begging were enough for them to allow us time for other ships. This travesty plaid out as you can imagine. We arrived, by miracle, in New Orleans, after quite a while of navigating the seasonal weather and taking turns on the pump to keep ourselves from sinking.

Our stay in the capital of Louisiana had no other purpose than to wait out the events that had caused our departure. Therefore everybody was under the illusion that we would spend a few days here and return to our houses one day. I, a fan of music and playing the flute quite well, joined a group of other youngsters who plaid various instruments, and formed a little band which gave us a pleasurable and honest occupation, and which served as the center of a crowded and pleasant society. But bad luck sought me out the more fun I had; I started to spurt blood from my mouth with such abundance and frequency that two groups of accredited doctors whom I consulted were of the opinion that some mortal accident had befallen me, as they imagined the spilling had to do with this or that organ (it ended up being a stomach ulcer).

Despite this, it didn't affect me in the slightest, as I felt no pain or inconvenience of any kind. More so since the flow of blood never decreased in spite of all the treatments, and I resolved to return to Spain, not without first obtaining a wooden branch called Anacahuita by the indians, which is reputed by them to be a cure for hemorrhages of all types.

This admirable remedy, which consists of drinking at all hours of the day the concoction prepared from the juice of the wood of said tree, boiling its splinters in clean water until the volume fell by half, and I drank it which served to make me completely healthy after eight days of using it. I never again suffered anything similar in the twenty seven years since then to this day where I write these lines. And I'm also convinced, after having recommended this to numerous patients with success, that medical science is nothing more than a trick paid for by charlatanism and ignorance.

What's undoubtable is that it's been over two thousand years since people have been complaining that the language of medicine is indecipherable to the sick; that health always finds a thousand reefs to collide on; that various treatments, both good and bad, are sold for fortunes of gold, that all health systems have to first be exaggerated, and then demolished by its very own practice, lucky that there was not just one treatment which after being in vogue, could not be accused of sooner or later of those who had submitted to it, and lastly, that a simple diploma, unmerited at times, concedes the right to doctors to destroy everything without heeding to anyone; the law protecting them from the imprudence of a prescription that drives anyone who takes it straight to the grave. And even today we know that no government nor nation has regulated the medical field, also ridiculous. Since its being supported by the law of the highest social magistrate, it has not however organized itself so, to the same level as other fields, as the hierarchy in medicine does not guarantee the acts of any of its members.

The indians employ to this day in their medicines the same methods used by the two famous doctors of antiquity, Chiron and Esculapio. Experience is their only guide, as was for those two great men of medicine. And, according to the opinion of an eminent professor, the benefits of medicine began to diminish since Hipocrates introduced his oaths. Because fiction takes the place of simplicity, and his contradictory theories paved the way for the homicidal and diabolic inventions that decimate civilized society.

In the year 1832, taking advantage of the fact that two friends were going to Europe, as business called them to England, I partnered with them. We decided to make the trip by land to New York, uniting the fun and brief with certainty and comfort, and around September, for forty duros, which included room and board, we began our journey on the steamer Peruvian, towards Louisville, a distance of 1450 miles from New Orleans.

We navigated upstream at six knots, despite the current being another six and the depth being no more than forty fathoms in front of the city, and in the first leagues passing by a beautiful countryside covered by estates and immense plantations, we arrived at Baton Rouge, a city which occupies the sunny hillside of the first elevation you find during the trip. Otherwise the terrain is completely flat and quite marshy, inhabited for the most part by French and Spaniards.

Continuing on our course, we came to the mouth of the Colorado river (*modern day Red River*), which bathes this immense country with the finest cotton, and which abundantly produces sugar, Maiz and other fruits. This river is the last tributary of the Mississippi and its length is so considerable that its origin is in the Sierra de Tatos, forty leagues further than Santa Fe of New Mexico, and passes through different peoples who do much commerce through its waterways.

From here, the Mississippi extends in a series of lateral canals called Bayoux, which disperses the water during the flooding of the plains. Without them, not being able to divert the water towards the Gulf of Mexico and Lake Pontchartrain and Mobile, the magnificent estates of Louisiana, including New Orleans herself, would find themselves flooded on a regular basis. When the plains flood, the water level rises as much as forty feet.

The Mississippi river serves as a border for the state of Louisiana, which owes its name to having been discovered by the French during the reign of Luis XIV. The western part, with New Orleans, was ceded to Spain in 1773 via a secret treaty, to indemnify the many sacrifices it had made in 1761. Some years later, in 1801, without a doubt due to the one of the scoundrels from our government at the time, it was ceded to Napoleon. But when that colossus attempted to begin various grand projects there, a war broke out which led to the Peace of Amiens, and he ended up selling it to the Americans.

The main city of this state, New Orleans, was founded around 1718 or 1719 by the government of Bienville and his men, since an extraordinary storm had obligated them to establish themselves in the area, as the bay of Mobile, in which they found themselves, had been filled with sand. It's situated about 90 miles from Belize, which is one of the main points of entry into the Gulf of Mexico.

Its first inhabitants gave it the name which still stands, to perpetuate the legacy of Philip of Orleans. But despite all the efforts of the West India Company, to whom several tax exemptions were afforded in order to develop and colonize that land, they nevertheless experienced a miserable life there. And only when the government of these lands became not just a tyranny over them but an expression of their will, and at times their humble servants, was finally when this city and the state of Louisiana reached the apex of prosperity which it finds itself in. And the best thinkers today, see the day not far when New Orleans will become the most frequented port in the entire United States, despite its unhealthy climate.

Five or six miles below the city, between the estates named Rodriguez and Bienvenida, is the site where the Americans defeated the British on the 8th of January, 1815. With just five or six thousand men haphazardly formed, they defeated the twelve thousand commanded by General Packenham of Wellington's army, who paid with his life the audacity of underestimating his enemy.

General Jakson, captain of the republicans, displaid in those moments a certain valor, a firmness and an energy without which it would have been impossible to overcome the obstacles faced by his troops. He imposed martial law, and imprisoned a judge who invoked habeas-corpus for a member of the legislature who had protested against various measures taken by the general. Most admirable was, having reestablished law and order, the magistrate condemned the general, imposing a fine of 1000 duros for his breach of law - and it is no less extraordinary that he paid it as a civilian regardless of the traditional military tribunals.

In the city there are numerous spacious roads, uniform plazas, and a series of notable public buildings, in neighborhoods which to this day contain inscriptions dating back to the time of the Spanish government. The paving is good and the brickwork is about 6 feet wide. Temples are to be seen everywhere and of every denomination, since all are free to worship as they please. But The Cathedral, which is the most important, is Catholic, since most of the original population were Catholic as well as their descendents; and I met and did business with the famous Capuchino Fray Antonio de Sedella, a Cordovian, who died as parish priest at ninety some years of age after having started as the garrison chaplain in town established by the Viceroy of New Spain, around the year 70.

Father Antonio, which is how everyone called him, never gave up the habits, the long beard, and the sandals of his religion, even though later on it was no longer customary. With his exceptional dress, he went gray dedicating his life to doing good, and though he never made Bishop, he was considered the patriarch of the religion in that city, and as the founder of the churches that exist for the Christian faith.

Upon his death his body was on public display for three days. During those days, masses of people without distinction came to kiss his feet and shed a tear over his coffin as a final goodbye. And furthermore, I saw his robe being divided into thousands of tiny pieces to be distributed among the faithful, as no one wanted to be left without a memory of him, or better said, no one wanted to be left without a true relic. The three days having transpired, the Orleanseans suggested that the body pass through the city's main avenues, and thus it was, accomanied by a great crowd, the spaniards acting as pall bearers. It's impossible to describe what happened. The laments and tears produced a despondency so pervasive, and people hovered over the balconies and windows, seeing the inanimate body pass by, the profusion of flowers and laurel wreathes made it look like judgment day.

While this occurred, the local statesmen gathered, composed of men of all sects, and they repealed the law that prohibited one being buried in a church, and father Antonio was sepulchered in the one he presided over. Everybody attended his service, including the major businesses and all centers of commerce and government were closed. And when the remains of this man, loved by all, lay entombed in the pantheon built for this purpose, the legislators convened again and reinstated the law which they had just suspended.

Creoles are by and large refined and friendly, and they treat strangers with open arms, especially Spaniards, of whom they have good memories. As proof of this, I am pleased to write to you what Mr. Flint wrote in his geography „Whatever the reason may be, the yolk of the Spanish government was always easy and light upon the anglo-Americans that lived under it. And even to this day, the time when they ruled here is spoken of as the Golden century".

Having now paid the debt of gratitude I owed to the town that took me in at my most vulnerable, precisely when it looked like I would lose my entire fortune, let's continue the description of my travels, if only to note the peculiarities that we came upon in transit, which don't seem odd to me now as I relate to you my life story.

Continuing our pilgrimage, we entered Natchez, which is a beautiful villa built on a little hill which overlooks the eastern bank of the Mississipi, it was founded by the franciscans who constructed there Fort Rosalia, giving it the name it now bares, as that is the name the savages living around that territory. But such were the humiliations inflicted that they inflicted on the poor indians, by the commander and the officers of the stronghold, that they resolved to take revenge. Too weak themselves to realize their intentions, they convened with other tribes bordering themselves to behead each and every one of their oppressors. Having no almanac to divine at which time they should complete the general dismemberment, the tribes compromised by planting fifteen stakes in each of their respective fields, of which they would yank out one each day. On the day the last stake was removed, a large number of the conquistadors had their heads removed within the hour. The surviving indians avenged the deaths of their brothers, destroying the recently founded city, which would not be rebuilt for many years.

A few hours after passing the mouth of the Arkansas river, lying about 191 miles from New Orleans, we came upon a hut hidden away in the woods which indicated the sad conditions of its inhabitors, and walking briefly around the vicinity, while the boatman replenished his provisions of wood, we came across a stone next to the house of a gravesite, rustically adorned, with the following inscription:

"Here lies Jean Randolf, who was tossed into the river along this beach. Having found in his pockets a sum of 1,353 pesos in bank notes, we advise his family or he who believes it is his right, and with justification, to introduce himself to recover these." Immediately we headed to the door to see if such an act of integrity had been followed through, and a right old man greeted us, who even after having put notice of the death in the newspapers of neighboring states, even to that day still held the money, as nobody had come to reclaim it.

Admiring such integrity that has few peers, we boarded again our vessel and continued our journey, reaching a town of little importance named New Madrid. Without a doubt the name of the town got our attention, and coming into town inquisitively, we crossed paths with a Jesuit, who told us that the town was founded by Spaniards who still comprised the majority of residents, and who in 1812 survived an earthquake whose likes had never been seen which resulted in the river coming out of its banks, submerging the town and leaving no survivors among those who stayed.

Seventy four miles from this town, Madrid, you find the confluence of the Mississippi and Ohio rivers. And such is the violence with which these two powerful rivals crash that it offers the spectacular sight of having their courses nearly paralyzed for almost twenty miles before they meet.

From the confluence of these two rivers, which I'll say is about two thousand miles from New Orleans, we navigated up the Ohio and arrived at Paduca, where it joins the Tenesi river. There we noticed that many women smoking pipes. From there we went to Potosi, from Potosi to Palmira, Troya, Rome and Carthage, to arrive finally at Albani, where we had to disembark as at the point the river rapids were too strong to navigate. In carriage, then, we arrived in Louisville which is an important town serving as the key to the rest of Kentucky. By the way, at a certain distance from this city, which at the start of the century was nothing more than an observation post built by General Clark, is the town of Bardstown, inside which, in a Jesuit school, my unforgettable brother was educated.

In the state of Kentucky there are a great number of Yankees that have migrated from the western part of New York and Connecticut. They're like the Galicians of the United States. When they leave the house of their parents, they receive nothing more than a chair to sit on, a yoke of oxen, an axe and pickaxe. With just these tools they cross three, maybe four thousand miles, before definitely settling down. Afterwards, in general, they no longer hear word from their parents, nor their parents from them.

Cincinati, which we came upon right away, is a city which from the outset began to show signs of the grandness it is known for. Although Columbus is the capital of the state, Cincinati is the most populous, the most prosperous, the most commercial and most industrial. And due to her great agricultural productivity she has come to deserve the distinguished name of "Queen of the West."

The Ohio reaches all the way to Pittsburg where either the ice or the extraordinary shallowness of the waters create impediments to our traversing. Coming across the second of these two, we had to begrudgingly renounce our travel via waterway, it being more comfortable, fun, and safer, and also shortening the distance required, and cheaper, in favor of taking a seat in a cramped and dangerous carriage. We gathered our luggage, including a container of Chacolique (light wine from the Bascongadas) which had been sent to me by my father shortly before leaving New Orleans, and we continued on our path.

Four powerful horses driven by a half crazed conductor, that we had to swap out every hour, were in charge of taking us at breakneck speed on a poorly built road. We hit so many bumps and knocking into one another, that it produced a fatal movement, at some point during the day a reign snapped off from the vehicle, and at night our carriage was shook so hard that one of the crossbeams broke loose and we crashed. Several of us were injured and knocked unconscious. Among them were my companions Palacio (Don Manuel) and Don Joaquin de Errazu, leaving me with the most minimal of injuries and the container of wine unharmed.

As a consequence of this stumble we had to walk a whole league on foot, until we reached the first hamlet, they helped us rehabilitate our carriage and we were able to reach a town called Xenia. There they built us a new one, and we were able to ride out the storm, passing by Colombus the capital of Ohio, which communicates with New York via Lake Erie and counts among its towns Urbanam, Medina, Cadiz, Union and Batabia, - we gladly arrived at Weeling which belongs to the state of Virginia and bordered by Pennsylvania.

A short distance from Wheeling, the island of Blamerkasset grabs the attention of travelers due to its three mild length, it's beautiful fertility, and for the memory of a catastrophe which gave it its name.

An Irish gentleman, fleeing from the horrors of the revolution that engulfed his homeland in 1801 and finding refuge in America, came to this island with his entire family. Rich and lover of beauty, he converted it into a sort of paradise which he enjoyed until 1810 in which a horrific fire buried his only daughter under the ruins of the magnificent palace he had built there as his residence. And having abandoned the place of such pain, he became involved in a conspiracy whose objective was to destroy the Union of the States, having to flee at last back to Europe.

We left Weeling through a rather difficult and dangerous route. We crossed the Allegheny mountains, which has an abundance of oats, and we gladly observed an infinite amount of walnut, oak, chestnut, fern, fruit bearing trees and other plants that we had not seen since we had left Spain. And crossing a fertile country side, whose condition we found extraordinary, we arrived safe and sound at the capital of the Republic.

In Washington City, all of my anxiety about going to New York and from there embark on to Europe, was directed toward revalidating my status as American citizen, which, according to the law, I had acquired during my residence in the country."

And here Don Clemente drops off his pen, -his memoirs unfinished, and leaving us with the curiosity of having known by himself the final chapters of such an exciting and fiercely led life.

One must note the oddity that in the year 1833 during his trip to New York, that it appears as if he is ready to make the jump back to his homeland. But what's certain is that in his last lines, he is still in America, incomprehensively stuck, and right here we start to doubt: did he manage to cross the pond?: and if he did, was it necessarily the last time he returned?: did he come directly to Utrera?: Why?

The answer to this we can find in a letter that Don Clemente writes to his friend Don Jose de la Lastra which was found in his accounting book titled "Tras cornudos apaleados" (after thrashing losers). In it, towards the middle, it states that in the year 1829 his friend had repaid money owed and that Don Clemente was answering to his friend by remitting a netted amount of what was owed to each other, and as it turned out Don Clemente ended up being the debtor. Later on our "grandfather" says, after the course of the years, 1831 and 1832, he had written him several letters further but had received no response; in 1834 he went to Tuspam in person on the same mission, and even then he found out nothing; and during the years '35 and '36 the gestures that Don Jose de la Lastra made in his name failed likewise.

It's certain however that although Don Clemente did embark in New York, and maybe even returned to Spain as he had intended, he would then return to those shores. His arrival definitively must have been in 1837, or shortly afterwards, once finalizing the lawsuit that obligated Juncal to return to him 2,178 duros that he was approximately owed. His destination could have been Cadiz, the obligatory port of arrival for most traveling on the winds from the new continent. Whether it happened this way or not, what is obvious is that he headed straight for Utreran fields, influenced perhaps by the prosperity achieved there by his uncle Don Francisco de Gibaja Marroquin and his son, Don Simon, the actual landlord around that time. Proof of this is the delicious letter that, on the 27th of October of 1838, having just arrived, he writes to Doña Teresa Lopez Doriga, widow of Don Bernardino de Gibaja, asking for the hand of her daughter, Teresita.

"Aunt and Lady of Mine" says Don Clemente, "after having acquired a fortune in America capable of securing a respectable rank, I have returned to Spain resolved to find someone with whom to share the pains and pleasures of matrimony for the rest of my life. Since my age now requires it, and nature demands it, ...my feelings.

In Teresita I see great characteristics which I imagine would be necessary to be happy. And I would like for you, as surely you are interested in her having the fortune of many titles, to steadfastly examine my deeds and character at your convenience, and later to tell me if you consider me worthy of her hand, in which case I would be ready to marry her forthwith. Likewise, if it were to be against your wishes, I would renounce the idea at once; since, I repeat, I wish nothing without your approval.

In the interim, I implore you that whichever outcome happens, that there be no alteration among our longstanding relationship. I never take advantage of the confidence placed in me by others, and you are always able to count on my discretion and respect, remaining as your humble servant, *q.s.p.b.*"

How he met Teresita, is the same as asking yourself how he made it to Andalucia. It could have been the intention of his uncle Don Simon, who it is said called on his nephew for assistance, and she entered via a familial event of sorts. It's possible that he himself, wishing to establish himself in his own right, decided for this cousin of his, without their being public acknowledgement of a prior agreement. We suppose that this manner of dealing with life was not something abnormal during these times. What is certain is that Doña Teresa accepted the overtures of Don Clemente, and wedding preparations were underway.

The next step was to tidy up the estate of num 7. of the plaza, from the village of Utrera, property of Teresita, which would become the future residence of the newlyweds, and began construction wherein he would sink 30,000 reales, also with proceeds from the money of the bride. It's fair to say that although Don Clemente's wealth was not to be taken lightly, she also had wealth to reckon with (*tenia las espaldas al descubierto*).

Our above mentioned lady had been born in Sevilla, on the 2nd of September 1811. She was eight years younger than her groom, and third cousin in terms of consanguinity due to being daughter of Bernardina de Gibaja, as we have said. She lived in Sevilla with her mother, whom we believe was her only daughter as we have no evidence of their being any other sibling, and she had already inherited from her father a well healthy economy. Hers was the house in Utrera, whose rebuilding was being undertaken, the grain farm of 600 hectares in the countryside of that region named "Caseron", and three houses more in the city of Santander. In summary, her allotment contribution to the matrimony was of 1,099,044 reales, a quantity far superior to the 400,000 reales of the groom.

Everything was then ready for the ceremony, the necessary ecclesiastic dispensation had been received due to the consanguinity of the bride and groom, when the sad and unexpected news was received from Rasines of the death of Don Juan de la Cuadra, father of Don Clemente. One more time he had to give in before the requirements of his nomadic and adventurous circumstances and could not attend to the funerals, just as it was not possible for him to do so some years earlier, during his time in America, when his mother passed away.

In spite of everything the wedding was held. The 27th of April of 1839 they married in the chapel of Sagrario de la Santa Patriarcal Iglesia of Sevilla, and in this manner among joy and sadness, consistent with how his destiny had always been, we begin with what we could call the second half of the life of Don Clemente.

The abudance and strength of the andalusian countryside opens before his eyes, and another ocean, that of grains, would shine with as much brilliance as once did the Atlantic. A new way of life began to outline itself on his horizon as he learned the secrets of the earth. Of that loyal and thankful earth that would always remember him.

Don Clemente dreams of an empire and he goes after it right away, his insurmountable ability to focus his life towards action. In his mind he plans the key steps of his new operations. As a first measure, he buys the house adjoining his own, demolishes it, builds silos in its place, as well as warehouses, offices, and to market it, he gets permission from city council to construct an arch over Bohorquez street, which separated the house from his neighbors. He must not've suspected then that this same act would cause him confrontation with his new countrymen. Although the current construction was at the time accepted, later on, once the members of town council had changed, some of them, Don Joaquin Giraldez at their head, they repealed the previous agreement and asked for judicial mediation from the city of Sevilla that the previous permit be rescinded. According to them, the new arch clashed with the public image.

But, who imagines that Don Clemente is conformist? How can he not protest? In his mind such an injustice can't exist. It is not possible, after having spent so much money in order to pave and build up his street, something that had already been accepted, would now be pulled out from him. Therefore, he goes before the panel in Sevilla, and shows that the project, which is being led by the foremost architect of Sevilla, will not only not damage the street, but would in fact beautify it and would be a demonstration of the originator's good will. Nevertheless, what was never mentioned in this lawsuit was the tunnel under the street, that Don Clemente would need to build, and which apparently was not in the original agreement. Although the city had always intended to build this tunnel itself, they made it the inexcusable price to pay that he build it himself in order for them to accept his other proposals.

And suddenly, only four days after the decision, destined to become the dwelling of his mother-in-law, who still lived in Sevilla, he acquires in a public auction the local jail. The old jail and town hall he, of course, demolishes, as it was never his intention to lock up his mother-in-law, and he rebuilds it giving it a sumptuous and distinct facade.

Already at these times, just barely having returned, his personality was being noted by his fellow citizens. His interest in culture (he researches the history of Utrera) as well as music and the arts in general (he helps start the creation of a philharmonica), as well as his own political ideas, are more than sufficient motivation for individuals of diverse backgrounds to be drawn to him. But at the same time, it's the same reason that an incipient opposition would align itself against him, which would grow in tandem with the growth of his influence.

His main project of establishing a grand estate now is in sight and he will not waste the opportunity. On the 15th of May of 1840, he buys a farm called the "ship of the Ballesteros" and 505 bushels from the "Meadow of the Garzos", both on the outskirts of Utrera.

These are times in which the whole of Spain is enjoying respite from the Carlista war, the one in which General Espartero is considered a national hero. In the neighborhood pubs, in the inns, and in the retail shops you would always see a portrait of his popular image. The liberal regime remained definitively secure.

Utrera also joins this fray. The plaza around the Villa changes names, and from then it would be called Duke of Victory. Don Clemente is euphoric. He, who is a true liberal, the most liberal in Utrera according to Manuel Marin Campos (so says an article published in the magazine "Utrera's Peak" in September 1963), sees now that the progressives are in power, those predisposed to publicly declare their convictions. But at the same time, a new chapter is going to open in his life. A chapter full of contradictions. In a few years he will undergo the most remarkable events that can affect a man's life.

Nineteenth of May, 1842, after having waited three years, his first son is born, Enrique Manuel Maria de los Dolores. But this joy is quickly tempered by the death of his mother-in-law, on the 25th of March of the following year, due to an inability to overcome a bout of pneumonia. She passes away at house six of the plaza of Duke of Victory, the very same one her son-in-law had remodeled for her. Soon thereafter their second son would be born, Federico, just before throwing himself in the bullring of politics. These are moments in which the interests of the parties and the political factions relegate to second position the interests of the community at large; in which justice shines due to her sheer absence, and in which taxes are redistributed according to political party and the common folks see themselves destined to redundancy as a result of their ideology. In these moments, we say, in which nobody speaks the truth and what the previous generation had built is destroyed, without realizing the loss, a group of neighbors emerges, with Don Clemente at the forefront, swearing an oath to each other to fight this off; all agreeing to dispense with their own political ideologies and enlist under one banner; Utrera.

Towards this goal they go about preparations for the coming electoral campaign, making among other things, detailed lists of those responsible for injustices mentioned, and on 9th of March of 1844 their delegate is selected and Don Clemente becomes mayor. And with the same gusto that follows all these endeavors, he takes office just three days later, and begins his tenure which will last two years. Because since the collapse of Espartero and the rise to power of the moderates, the party of Cuadra declined and he lost interest in participating in national politics, and his position as mayor became less influential, as a government of moderates and conservatives could not tolerate a liberal mayor.

During this time he denounced and corrected the vices that the administration he now ran had been perpetrating and at the end of his mandate, to clarify his actions before the public, he writes and publishes a memoir and general ledger of his office and activities, and seeing as how unexpected this was, and clearly stated, it was eagerly read by the public. It was said at the time that, being one of the most respected actions that he could've done not only for Utrera but as an example to the other towns in the province. It was such that, more than just a memoir of his tenure, it can be considered a public treatise for what can be accomplished by an officeholder with righteousness of principles, energy and firm will.

But before having crossed the median of his time in office, death itself was stalking around those parts. The 12th of October, 1844, one year after her mother and to the same disease - Teresita will pass away, his wife, when she had barely reached thirty three years of age. Truly we must recognize that life had been cruel to our "grandfather", cruel and sadistic. He had barely had the time to fill his wounded heart when it was torn apart violently, forcing him to begin healing anew. Since he was a child he had had to learn how to overcome hardship. Never before had he lost the will to live, not even in the most trying times. But this time was different. He faced a different enemy: an emptiness. He soon finds himself alone, fallen, with two children who had barely begun to live and whom would rely solely on him. It must've been a situation of extreme anguish, and terrible for a man of his age and character. Those boys must have troubled him greatly, as nowhere in his life experiences had he faced such a challenge. The only answer was the refuge of his family. He searches for help from his sister Feliciana, who lived in Racines with her daughter Prudencia, and she responds with every possible effort to care for his children (he brought them on the first railway that was inaugurated in Spain, Barcelona-Mataro in 1848) and with a great determination of spirit. She would raise them for many years as her own children, and this would incur her the well-deserved appreciation of our forefather who had to return to Utrera to take care of his public obligations.

Let's return then to politics, and let's explore the consequences of those two years as head of the town council of Utrera. Just to be clear, in those years he had no more powers than previous administrations. Although it's true that taxes were levied on the sale of hard liquors and the office of weights and measures was rented out, it's certain that one or another tax was destined to the cemetery first, and to the jail second. At the end of the day the economy of the town had neither been expanded or diminished. And those who were opposed to these taxes had lacked standing, and one could not argue against the new projects being indispensable. Above all, in those times when people were buried – the cadavers were interred in the city, in the crypts of the Churches, or in the outskirts where the bodies were robbed, and the existing jail was a veritable meat grinder of which anyone who considered themselves a humanitarian would be ashamed to see. The new one, however, had an infirmary, workshop, etc. by way that its inhabitants could become socially rehabilitated through labor. It was perhaps an example that Utrera gave to Spain, of a vision of prisons that would nevertheless take many years to be adopted in the rest of the country.

Another important subject to touch upon was that of public sanitation. Utrera had an open air market, in the middle of a street, spaces which lacked the most basic hygienic elements. In spite of this, nobody believed it necessary to build a more adequate infrastructure, which caused the greatest opposition to his administration during his tenure. Some said that the envisioned market was small and poorly situated; others, that a new market would require additional needless taxes; and the rest, engaged in corrosive and bitter arguments designed to abort the project.

Despite it all, this group of men would not be discouraged. The market ended up being built without the creation of any taxes, the only money being used from a well-run budget, and those who were against the project found themselves at a loss.

Regarding urbanism, something else to understand, still today we have the public walkways and construction and paving of the Plaza Mayor. And since the facade of the Villa had a lot to be desired since a good bit of the town had been abandoned and vacant, we had what could be called the creation of alms houses. Several of them were purchased between the council members and the mayor, they were gutted and rebuilt, in order to later be sold among the neighbors, thereby recooperating the invested money. And this was accomplished rather quickly, says Don Clemente, in but little time we managed to change the landscape of our town. But again, in this instance, they prayed for those families bereft of wealth, and at the same time were able to improve the condition of some of their neighbors.

Finally, so far we know, the old problem of education was not ignored, which was about to be resolved when Doña Juana Gonzalez Rice, who upon her death, gifted the Jesuits the necessary means to build a school nearby. But it turns out that before this could occur, the confiscations of Mendizabal came about (countrywide seizure and sale of church lands) and dispossessed them, and with that dispossessed Utrera's youth from the inheritance of Dña Juana. Since then all the succeeding municipal administrations had taken up the cause, to no avail. Despite even, two decrees from Maria Cristina (Queen of Spain) during the years '41 and '42 in their favor. And in these moments, the administration run by Cuadra had to retreat from the law as a new decree had been issued which contradicted the decrees of previous years. And although Don Clemente won't see the lawsuit resolved during his tenure, years later when the matter had finally settled in their favor, he helps with the inauguration of the school, of that old and cramped building which still existed, tired from the forging of generations of Utrerans.

And from all of the projects he undertook as mayor, he left a detailed record of accounts with his signature on each and every page, so that nobody would take credit for his work nor seek to make false claims of him later on. And ending his years in that capacity, he exhorts his fellow townsfolk to continue improving the city in subsequent administrations, and to not be taken in by promises but to watch for actions. These are the wishes of a man who expresses his advice to his neighbors in a testament.

It appears that his duties to his town didn't cease when he left the office he'd been elected to, in fact his leadership was in demand more than ever. But his intention had always been to hand things off to others, and in that moment or shortly thereafter, he returns to Rasines to live with his sons. It's simply a move of headquarters for him. From there he would continue to direct and grow his business in Utrera, where he no doubt expected to return one day when the circumstances permitted. Because the day that he left to America, his hometown had become a memory. A fond memory of course, but if not for these special circumstances, perhaps he would never have returned. Nevertheless, there he would stay until the year 1866. Almost twenty years of his life!

With his fame for being a rich adventurer, Don Clemente enters Rasines finding the doors of all his family and friends wide open. This support and warm welcome which they showed him greatly strengthened his dedication to developing his business and interests. At the center of gossip and discussion within the town, he would go about slowly rediscovering it, sensing in every corner the throb of memory from his distant childhood. He would meet his relatives, the majority whom he would be meeting for the first time.

Some of them came to be good friends of his, like Don Jose Maria Lopez Doriga, uncle of his deceased wife, whom he appreciated greatly and who he would later name, along with Don Simon, as mentors for his sons in the will that he drew up in Santander on the 17th of June of 1853.

At first it appears that he lived with his sister Feliciana. But some time later (1851), when it appears that his stay there will be lasting, he buys two houses in the *cerro* neighborhood, he renovates them, links them together and prepares himself for the move. Little by little he realizes the reality of his new situation.

He learns then, of the lands he will inherit from his father, and goes about acquiring several more, although small and spread out. In sum he managed to have there the equivalent of 374 hectares, six houses in different places, two mills and one ruined forge. However, the majority of his businesses were related to his fields in Utrera. His goal of creating a giant plantation continued apace. Besides, by then after the inheritance from his mother, his sons now owned an important part of the estate; and for them – it was for them, those who had little desire for the quiet life of the Santander mountains, he prepared that grand plantation. The opportunity comes from the times. These are the years following the famous decree by Mendizabal and the recent Madoz law. And, as the first one regulated the disbandment of the massive ecclesiastical estates and the second the communes, nobles were allowed to sell up to half of their inherited estates, there was now an abundance of investments and Don Clemente, as others of his day who were possessed of economic possibility, was one of the beneficiaries of this transfer of ownership. This way the new andalucian latifundios (gigantic agrarian estates) were created thus clearly demonstrating the failure of the politics of government.

The 13th of April of 1849 he acquires the fields of Pabellon Grande y Encinilla through a public auction, in amount ultimately measured at 440,000 reales in copper – the 13th of July of 1858, the 99 bushels of grain from the Meadow of the Garzos and 18 days later, the fields of Troya y la Cañada, all adjacent to the original field, Caseron. It's then that he decides to fund in Rasines, where they still reside, a school for girls, which at that point did not exist. Since he's convinced, as he himself tells us, that:

"Ignorance is the cause of society seeing itself invaded by corrupt individuals when people lack the education necessary that would soften their habits, remove them from vices, and incline them towards vocation and work. In this sense I want to leave nothing to be desired; the youth here have a complete education – due originally to the generosity of my relatives Don Francisco de Gibaja and Don Andres Gil de la Torre. For my part, figuring it was the highest good I could do for the town where I was born, once its poverty had been attended to, is the establishment which I solely funded, so that orphaned girls could receive an education free of charge that is worthy of their august mission bequeathed to them by nature."

The school was granted on the 20th of October, 1858, and the new school would be located facing the parochial church, having a rent of 1,666 reales per year which Don Clemente himself would pay for from his Encinilla field, and even to this day the school exists and in the entrance one can see a memorial stone to this act. In 1860, the good and single Don Simon, who had reached 63 years of age, falls sick in his home in Utrera. He calls for Don Antonio de Campo Redondo y Rosnotario de la Villa, to take his final will of his goods. That decision could not have been better timed, for the next day, 1 June 1860, he dies of stroke at his house on Calle de La Hermosa, num 33.

The assets of Don Simon were approximated to be more than 3,623,798 reales, of which 2,021,743 were figured in precious metals. Of these, he willed 853,011 in the following way:

- 64,000, as a stipend for 8,000 masses at 8 reales a piece.

- 360,000, to hand over to Don Manuel Pico Gil, for his good work.

- 240,000 to his loyal and old maid, Dolores Ortega

- 120,000 to be split among the nieces of the latter, Ana and Dolores Espinel.

- The remainder for burial costs, funds for two convents in Utrera, and other uses which honor him and give testament to his good heart.

To his nephews Enrique and Federico he leaves them 146,091 reales in precious metals to each one, 113 hectares of olives, 4 vineyards, and the house on the calle Hermosa, of which he states his wish that Don Manuel Pico Gil and Dolores Ortega continue habitating it, his faithful servants – without paying rent at all, until Don Enrique had turned twenty five years old.

And to his other nephews, Don Juan, Don Francisco, Doña Rosario, Doña Consuelo, Doña Ramona de Gibaja Bengochea, - children of his deceased brother Don Santiago, he leaves them all and equal amount of 146,091 reales, and the farm at Merrera in the outskirts of Utrera.

Some days later, the 18th of July, they went before the notary to sign the papers settling the estate of Don Juan de Gibaja Bengochea, those in his name and those of his brothers, Don Clemente who had arrived from Rasines, in the names of his sons, and as executors Don Manuel Pico Gil, from Utrera, Don Ignacio de Viya, cousin of Don Clemente, and neighbor in the town square of Cadiz.

After a few years, in 1866, following the custom of the time and carried by the pragmatism of his character, our "grandfather" decides to search for adequate girlfriends for his sons. Don Enrique is destined to be with a young lady having just arrived from Mexico, named Marciala Sainz de la Maza y Gomez de la Puente, who according to reports had been generously blessed by nature. Federico on the other hand had worse luck. It's known that he complained to his brother and he resisted the idea of such an imposition on him at all.

Enrique and Marciala set the date for the 27th of February, 1867 in Rasines, and although the groom had not reached the age of majority (25 years), his father tells him that it is now time to participate (and Federico too) in the responsibilities that are his to administer to. But although these are his words, it doesn't appear to have occurred this way.

At the hour of truth, this remains just a theory. Don Clemente doesn't release the reigns so easily. He's already 64 years old, but far from feeling the fatigue of the continual struggle, he appears to continue to have all the strength in the world to keep at it. And you could almost believe that his return to Utrera (1867) would rejuvenate him and breathe new spirit into him. Just as he returns, he buys another farmhouse named "Berlobrego", along with 317 hectares, the estate "Haza Grande" near the edges of the village of Moron and the farmlands Torecillas at public auction. All of this he adds to another property "Alorin", that he had acquired a year before, and being on the borders of his other properties, like the Berlobrego, totals among them all a grand estate surpassing over 600 hectares of "Caseron" in addition for a total of 5013 hectares.

Once Don Enrique is married he installs himself in the house on Calle De La Hermosa, which he inherited from his uncle Don Simon, and his father (Clemente), who did not wish to live in his prior residence at the Plaza de la Villa, of such sad memories, buys the houses numbers 21 and 23 on street Garci Gomez (16-4, 1868), and he goes about renovating them. He wants to build himself an adequate home, and he wishes to also leave a plaza before his house to draw distinction. To do so he asks permission of the town council, and he's determined to cover all of the costs required to build it, and pass it over free of cost to the city. The only condition being that within it a memorial stone be placed showing the name "Plaza de Gibaja" and for this name to never be changed under any ecclesiastical, civil, military, nor any other at all. And in case this were to happen, Don Clemente in his will of 22 May, says that the property would revert back to its origin, passing along to the property on 33 on the Calle De La Hermosa, from which it is was carved from. The next day, 23 May of 1868, the town councils accepts the offer unanimously, along with its conditions, and he goes about the task of demolishing the existing structures, and goes about slowly discovering the dirty conditions of the properties 25 and 27 of the street Garci Gomez: these properties are acquired likewise (30 July 1868), are torn down, and then are reborn as the houses marked number 2 of Plaza de Gibaja; number three, where Don Clemente is to live, the number three having a lower floor with the door opening to the street, destined to contain warehouses, grocery stores, and granaries; and the number 1, the prior number 33 on the Calle De La Hermosa.

Our "grandfather" being customarily impassioned and fully engrossed in the above task, his son Federico falls ill – he had returned from Belgium having finished his studies as an Agronomist. The sickness is extremely grave, the doctors diagnose him with Meningitis. And Don Federico dies single, at age 24, the 15 of November of '68, without having left a testament to his will.

In the middle of everything, Don Clemente does not cease his business activities and doesn't know when to go about diminishing his acquisitions. Despite his age and his adversities he never considers it opportune to abandon himself to his well deserved rest. Only fifteen days had gone by since the passing of his son and already he is finalizing the terms of a contract to buy several vineyards in the reaches of Montellano and in Coronil (9-XII 1868). Afterwards, he goes about new acquisitions, primarily olive fields, in Utrera, Montellano and Lebrija. His last purchase, the 16th of August of 1871, a house sporting the number 5 on the Calle Nueva, in the town of Coronil, bought from Don Diego Villalon Gonzalez, Marquee of Pilares.

At these heights, whether from being conscious of his age or from starting to feel the logical exhaustion of such an unyielding life, Don Clemente wishes to pen his will, spelling out certain partitions which his later circumstances made necessary. He adds from his fist and pen a clause, in effect stating "his uncles Don Juan Lopez Doriga and Don Simon de Gibaja having died, before writing their wills, like his son Don Federico, a name universally inherited by Don Enrique. And in case the latter passes away before taking possessions of the assets, all is to pass to the grandchildren Fernando, Teresa, and any other having been later born, their cousin Don Andres Martinez de la Cuadra should be the executor. He also adds that it is his will that, for his son or he who represents him, shall turn over ten reales on a daily basis to his sister Feliciana and to her daughter Prudencia, as long as they live, as his appreciation for the care they always demonstrated towards him, and the love with which they helped rear his children. He also notes that should Feliciana and her daughter become separated or impoverished, they are free to live in his house in the Plaza de Gibaja or in the one in Rasines in the Somellera neighborhood, and they should do so without paying rent at all. But if his son Don Enrique should wish to live in this last house, they should rather occupy the house that is situated across the street in the same place.

Afterwards, he signs and later rewrites it again nearing the epilogue of his life, he brings clarity in a new clause where he funds a new school for girls in his home town, and arranges for it to be free of tuition to girls and for the teachers to be paid.

In the year 1873, going on nearly 70 years of age, a stubborn companion of his life gave him the irreversible date. The 7th of February, at the onset of night he dies of cerebral apoplexy in his house on Plaza de Gibaja. His eyes closed, the beats of his heart had stopped, and forever gone was his presence. But there remained on the earth his work sprung from years of work and longing. Firm and unforgettable through the ages just like the statue that I saw.

About the Author

Steven Nelson spent his childhood in Spain playing with cousins in the rubbles of the castle belonging to the Cuadra family. At age 10 he moved to the U.S. and went on to study Business and History, including a year as a student in Germany. Fascinated with storytelling since a boy, he has written numerous works of historical fiction, diving into the past for inspiration. His first published work is the authentic, translated manuscript of his Spanish ancestor's memoirs from the 1800s. Next we will follow a band of fellows in the early Middle Ages, a fascinating time of barbarian invasions, clashes between cultures, the slow fall of Rome, and for being known by that abused name: "the Dark Ages."

More than anything he wants his reader to awaken in a bygone world that after so long still reaches out to us today. He is experimenting with interactive fiction, giving the spotlight to you, the reader, to face the moral conundrums of the heroes and take responsibility for the lives of our protagonists. Steven Nelson has worked as a language teacher, waiter and currency trader, living of late in Cincinnati.

www.ingramcontent.com/pod-product-compliance
Lightning Source LLC
Chambersburg PA
CBHW031627040426
42452CB00007B/708